Driven to Drive

Success Tips for a Professional Driving Career

By Bruce Outridge

Dedicated to the Professional Truck Driver

Copyright Information

Driven to Drive is published by Bruce Outridge Productions a division of Outridge Enterprises inc.
Mailing Address:
Outridge Enterprises Inc.
700-20 North Shore Blvd West
Burlington, Ontario, L7T 1A1

Written and illustrated by Bruce Outridge
Online purchases available at www.outridge.ca |
www.outridgeenterprises.ca and other approved retailers.

To purchase copies by phone please call 289-337-2630

ISBN Number: 978-09919625-2-5

Inside the Book

Introduction

This book is the second book based on the transportation industry that I have been a part of for over 30 years. Even though I am no longer driving, I am still very involved with the people in the industry and development for new drivers. The first book titled Running By The Mile focuses on the business end of operating a truck and becoming your own boss. By itself it makes the book somewhat intimidating to those that want to just be a driver and that is where the foundation of Driven to Drive came from.

If there is one thing that gave me a long satisfying career in transportation it has been leadership and owning my career. I have vowed to control it the best I could by being involved and working hard. That work ethic has taken me to great heights in my career that many other drivers have only wished for. I have always made good money in the industry, driven great equipment, and met many awesome people. Today I do my best to pass on the same techniques and work ethic that made me a respected professional driver. To make it even more fun I have interwoven many different stories that have happened to me during my career in somewhat of a chronological order so that you can see not only how my career progressed, but help you realize that many opportunities are there and you may not notice them. This book is meant to be a guide only and is not meant to be a bible of how to become a professional driver. It is more a book on how I did it; hopefully it will give you some ideas that will help you in your career.

Every career will be different and every story will be different, how you handle it is the real point of the book. I hope this book inspires you to step up to the plate in your career and be the best you can be. One thing I found is that you can really improve your future by taking hold of some of the opportunities available, for instance I wouldn't have thought about how much my moving career taught me about Customer Service but it was one of the best training environment I found for truck drivers. Every company I have been with has taught me something different that added a different skill set to my so called "tool box". This book is set to help you realize the importance of customer service in your career, learn how becoming an ambassador to the industry can take your career to great heights, and how it doesn't matter where you are in your life right now, you have the tools to go forward and have a successful career. I believe the most important thing I am hoping to show with this book, is the importance of the transportation industry and what a great career it can be. This is not a career for people who can't do anything else as previously thought; this is not an industry of cowboys, and wild people. It's funny that people in a car will judge a truck driver's actions on the roadway, but when they sit in a truck they are amazed at the talent required to keep that truck going safely down the highway. Driving a tractor trailer takes great skill and is not something that is done without talent, common sense, training, and coordination. That can't be done by some drug-eyed maniac driven cowboy. I am not saying we don't have the odd one, but they don't last in our industry very long, taking the profession seriously, operating professionally, and planning on a long career path that grows as you do is the way to operate in the world of transportation. I have made many mistakes but in the end I can look back on my career and consider it a success. I want you to have the same success that I have had in my career, but you have to have one thing, determination! You have to be Driven to Drive!

Enjoy the book,
Bruce Outridge

This is not a career for people who can't do anything else as previously thought; this is not an industry of cowboys, and wild people.

Chapter 1
Driven to Drive

They read every report card, they all said the same thing, if Bruce would only pay attention. Each report card comment seemed to be a carbon copy of the comment ahead of it. I didn't know anything about passion back then, what it could do for you, why you would want it, or even what it was. We all have them and some recognize them and others don't or keep them inside just wishing they had the motivation to keep them moving forward. As a kid you may have had passions that kept you moving forward. I just know that throughout my school life it was a consistent trail of "no" that seemed to keep me at levels that would only attract the homeless. I was a terrible student. I found out the one thing I was good at was the one class I didn't like or take, and that was art. I loved to draw, in-fact it was the first passion I realized was a passion and participated in it without being pushed to do it, I would spend hours drawing and copying other artist that I found in the paper and in magazines. Even then I didn't know how it would shape me later in my life. Passion has a way of making you better and I would find that out later in life throughout a successful trucking career, but channeling that work wouldn't come for a long time. It was shortly after I began working odd jobs that passion for the job and money worked hand in hand.

Being brought up with a good work ethic is probably one of the best things that my parents ever gave me, it helped groom my career, it helped me stand above the rest and it helped me gain the integrity that can take you through life allowing you the opportunities to be successful. My parents were smart enough not to allow me to just get money without working for it, I am sure looking back because they didn't have it, we were middle class, but not rich by any means. My parents came from Guyana in South America the year before I was born so they were not born into the landscape of North America with large roads, big trucks, and large equipment. My dad worked many odd jobs from car wash to cabbie to make a buck before moving into the accounting field that kept him for the rest of his life. They taught me to keep a job you had to work hard. What I found out through those days of odd jobs as a teen is that if you want to make money, enjoy your work and that still rings true to this day. My days of flipping hamburgers, and making fries were great. I worked with some great people that liked to have a good time and have a boss that wasn't afraid to laugh and treat us with respect. As kids we have all played the game of a sore stomach to stay away from school, but in those days I never remember phoning in sick to work, I loved being there. I worked many odd jobs through high school from fast food cook to gas station attendant. All the time being groomed for a life in transportation that I didn't even see coming. Were you one of those kids that played in your parents car pretending to drive or on the family tractor on the farm? The driving may be in your blood. I didn't realize that those times sitting in my Dad's Corvair while parked in a closed garage was shaping me for a life in trucking. The best was when I went out with Dad alone to the store or on some menial errand he would put me on his lap and let me hold onto the wheel that he was mentally reaffirming my love of driving. I didn't know any of that, all I knew is that there was a certain freedom with a vehicle that allows you to go where ever you want. I was being groomed, and transportation would be the route of my passion. The age of sixteen couldn't come fast enough, I remember the count down as if it was yesterday, I even had my Mum on standby to take me to the vehicle test centre on my birthday to write my as we called it "365" which was a temporary permit for a year. I had saved money from working and enrolled in a driving course right away. I even lucked out with the driving company as I was assigned to an instructor that used his own car and that car was a Camaro.

How cool was that? I am not terribly religious but the Lord has a way of enhancing your passions from above. I loved to drive and my instructor told me I was good at it, a message I wasn't told through my teachers at school so I thrived in the vehicle. My Dad sold me many old vehicles at that time, but it taught me that with my own car I could go anywhere, and I did. That passion for driving would make me successful later, but would be the detriment of my high school career at the time. Passion has a way of coming to the surface however, and mine would show its head again and soon. Those couple of years would be a roller coaster ride for me,I was doing badly in school if I was there at all, work was on and off and I was partying way too much for a kid that age. Going back I think the ages of sixteen to eighteen had to be some of the worst years of my life. I had good times, but many bad times as well, times that I didn't really understand. Without knowing it my passion for driving started to move me in what I thought was the wrong direction in life. I was barely going to school and so at the ripe old age of seventeen I dropped out of school. I would spend more time driving around school than attending it and the scene wasn't getting any better. In the 70's it was a time of revolting against your parents and I seemed to be at the helm, often for no reason other than it seemed convenient.

Dropping out of school was like retirement for me, lay around wondering what to do with my day, I had a small part time job that was paying the gas for my car so I spent much of my time doing things like roller skating day and night and partying with friends. The truth is I didn't know what I wanted to do. Unknown to me trucking would soon come calling. My Dad's motto was if you weren't in school, you were at work and for a couple of months he had to drag me out of the house to find a real job. I got a job selling encyclopedias that didn't last very long. I found a job doing construction work which I didn't like and finally ended up working for an agent for Atlas Van Lines.

I was a big kid in high school and so carrying furniture out of the house was a great job for me. I loved it, I became very good at the job although the company was struggling at best. The equipment was pretty basic and all the fuel was paid with cash. Normally in a moving company the tractor trailer drivers are considered the top drivers and everyone falls underneath them. I was instructed one day to go with the senior driver Dave to Windsor to pick up a load of furniture going state side. We had this old Brigadier tractor that had a top speed of around 50 miles and hour. We were given $50 for fuel as the bean counter boss had figured out the mileage to the place and how much fuel we would need to get there and back. Driving four hours away and back seemed a lot farther than fifty dollars would take us, but it was diesel fuel and heck what did I know. What the brain wave boss didn't plan on was a head wind equaling the speed of our truck or the extra weight of the load allowing us to run out of fuel shortly after leaving the customer. back then there were no cell phones so it was a long walk to make that call for more money. I have been in the business for over thirty years and that is the last time I have ever run out of fuel in a truck. Some experiences have a lasting effect in the opposite ways. My passion however, was creeping back into the picture.

"Hope I don't get a head wind!"

I wasn't driving yet but was watching what the other drivers were doing. In a moving crew the driver is usually the boss of the crew on site, he seemed to not lift as much furniture as the rest of us because he was loading the truck, and they got to relate to the customer more. I was intrigued with the position and started to ask questions and take notes of the steps needed to drive a truck. Back then you could just take a written test if you had a car license and begin driving if another licensed driver was with you. So that's what I did, I wrote the test and began to drive the small trucks from the agent. Passion has a way of bringing out the best in people although the work was hard I was enjoying it. I shined in this area, I liked to drive, I liked dealing with the people for the most part, and I was a good leader with the crew. If I had to single out one thing that best outlined what I enjoyed the most about the job would be the freedom. I enjoyed going to different places everyday, meeting new people, and seeing different homes and lifestyles. I have moved many people over my time in the moving industry, some well known authors in Toronto, to hockey stars and more.

The art of customer service!

The moves I remember the most however are the bad ones, like the time we showed up at a home for a local move and nothing was packed. We used to hate those moves as they dragged on and would take much longer. This one however would not take us as long since when we arrived the women told us she was leaving her husband, he didn't know, he came home for lunch every day, and he owned a gun. You have never seen a truck loaded so fast, it was a whirl wind of activity. Then there was the time that we couldn't get the couch into this small basement so the man of the house brought out a giant chain saw and cut the couch in half in the front yard. If only he had known I was joking when I said we should cut it in half. Most of the time however I have enjoyed meeting people and they have provided me with the best training for a truck driver, dealing with the public.

In the moving business the work slows to a crawl in the winter time. There are very few house moves and most of the work is either warehouse work or working with other drivers. All the other able bodies would be laid off until spring so the lesson there is if you want steady work have a license and be good enough they don't want to lose you.

"If you want steady work have a license and be good enough they don't want to lose you."

I had received my "D" license by this time and when work was slow I would either work with this guy Al who seemed to have some type of stomach problem but refused to do anything about it. We would repack containers with furniture from storage customers and as Al walked he would fart. As the person trailing him let me tell you I didn't find this funny or enjoyable. To get away from this I would offer to go out with the tractor trailer drivers whenever possible. I was happy to get out of the warehouse and since I was a good mover the drivers were happy to take me a long. At that time I didn't realize I was getting my first introduction into the world of trucking, but a driver Ray would be the introduction to a world that I would remain in for the next 25 years of my career.

I had only been in a tractor trailer a few times at this point and it was that old Brigadier General that ran out of gas so heading out with Ray was a big deal. He had a giant Kenworth with no bunk but it sat high on it's frame. You could see everything, I was amazed. We were headed to Ottawa at that time and the trip seemed like we were driving to Florida. I was told to be at the yard for 5 in the morning to beat traffic. I was so green, we were going for the day, so we would be driving five hours one way, delivering the furniture, and then returning back to Mississauga. Log books weren't used in Canada at that time and you could run as long as you wanted to. I'll never forget the blinding light, it was like we were driving into the sun, I struggled to keep my eyes open, and all I could hear was Ray laughing in the driver's seat saying why didn't you bring any sunglasses? I eventually fell asleep and woke up as we pulled into some truck stop for breakfast. Although I didn't know it this would be my first introduction to business. In the moving industry many times you need at least one other person to help you unload the truck. Van line owner operators have the option of hiring help at the closest agent to their customer, but regional drivers such as Ray often just cut deals for their favourite helper.

This was beneficial to them because they knew who they were getting as far as help and if you got someone good you only had to hire one person instead of two. This is where I got quite a bit of work even when not driving. The driver would negotiate with something like paying you one hundred dollars for the day and all your meals, this way they didn't have to pay for traveling time in the truck. Unless you had your own money and many of us didn't back then if you forgot to negotiate meals you probably weren't eating that day. That one trip to Ottawa pushed my passion for the road even deeper, I knew this is what I was meant to do, I loved the travel, the freedom, the trucks, everything, it was great. The farther your passion is ingrained in you the better you will be at the job, therefore you will make more money. The key part is you will enjoy doing the work and will be willing to invest more time in your career.

In transportation very often we tell young drivers don't skip around in your careers too much because it gives the impression of a shoddy work record, that you can't be relied on for the long term and so on. I agree that as you move further and further into your career your employment should increase in years, but if you started like me moving up the ranks of professional was more important. That's what begun to happen, I had reached the two year mark of working at the Atlas Van Lines agent in Mississauga. I had started at the age of seventeen, I had acquired my "D" license and had put two years of experience behind me moving from lumper to driver. The problem was that the agent wasn't really big so I only drove when someone else didn't show for work or there was an emergency delivery. I also learned that my boss was a control freak, they say he wanted to be a Police Officer but couldn't get in, thank you Lord for that, I think he would have been more dangerous on the street. I felt stifled there and at that point you have to decide if it is time to move on. They had taught me what to do and what not to do, but I felt it was time to move on so I moved to North American Van Lines, the agent was a little larger with newer equipment and a good steady base of work. This was also my first lesson into the challenging world of egos. I happened to apply at the right time as a new larger straight truck was open for a driver.

It was brand new with brand new equipment and I would be dedicated to this truck. I loved the truck and remembered the lessons I had learned earlier that customer service is everything, and that meant from the time you opened the doors of the truck. I was meticulous with this truck laying down a pattern that would last the rest of my driving career. The existing drivers didn't like it however, they felt threatened probably because they stopped growing. When you stop growing in a position you are dead. It is the same in business as an entrepreneur, if you stop growing your business you start to decline in the opposite direction. The other drivers stopped growing and started with this "I've been here longer" crap that makes them look like a great big babies. Many came to accept me but one bucked the system the whole time until he had enough and quit. That was his problem not mine and I became one of the star drivers at the agent. I learned if you just do your job to the best of your abilities everything will fall into place. Every time I have seen someone buck the system in my career they usually end up leaving when they see they aren't getting anywhere. They have decided to use their energy to sabotage and complain instead of staying on top of their game. Once you head down that path you usually start messing up which in turn affects customer service and then, bye bye.

I haven't been here too long, do I look old to you?

In trucking customer service is paramount to getting new business however most drivers miss the boat on this and wonder why they don't make more money than they do. Whether you deal with the receiver on the dock, the manager of the shipping department, your very own dispatch department, or the public, customer service should be your first priority. In moving having a good relationship with customers will move you up the ranks faster than being a great driver because that is the focus of the job. Driving the truck is only getting the freight or product from A to B, the real work is delivering and dealing with the clients. This training would set me apart from many of my colleagues because I figured that out early. I dressed appropriately even back when the movers were wearing old t-shirts and cut off jeans. I learned that professionalism made the customer more at ease and by doing that they gave me more respect allowing me more control of the job. If I made a suggestion about how to move a piece a certain way very rarely did I get backlash from the customer as they felt I had the knowledge to perform the task successfully. I have kept that close to me to this day. Customer Service starts at the office. Hopefully all information is handed down properly to the driver so they can arrive on time, but the driver must make sure they are on the ball, as they are usually the first person the customer meets. In trucking it is the small things that get you noticed, not the big things. Running over the customer's front lawn or taking out their favourite fir tree isn't going to make them feel better about putting their prized possessions on your truck.

Having moving pads thrown all over the back of the truck doesn't make them feel better about loading their furniture inside. Showing up without a piano cart when they specifically told the office they had a piano shows them communication break down in your company chain. I learned these lessons early and they helped me jump start to the head of the pack. I never left a customer until the truck was put back and organized the way I wanted it and the way a customer liked it.

Even things liked the pads had to form a nice line and look neat and orderly. They are strategically placed so that you use a certain amount of pads per square foot. This way you don't have to move them to create space for the furniture. When unloading the truck the drivers job is to pull the furniture down and fold the pads. Many helpers feel the driver should help and take furniture in the house so they offer to fold pads for me. Of course the answer was no, I would rather stay late and fold the pads myself as the truck had to look a certain way. This caused two of my helpers to take great action. We were on a move in the winter so it had been slow so all three movers on the move were experienced drivers. The fact was I had been scheduled for the move so it was my truck and I was the leader. As we were unloading the truck taking off the last few pieces I was doing my usual job of folding pads. I all of a sudden heard the doors close and the place went dark. I could hear laughing as I pounded on the inside of the truck for my so called associates to let me out. I then heard the engine start up and the truck start to move. Realizing I had been kidnapped by my own men I took a seat on a stack of pads.

"Let me out of here!!!!"

When the door reopened at the yard my two colleagues were on the ground laughing their head off. I myself was not as amused. It was a mutiny!

That level of customer service set a bar that I have never ducked under and always strive to push upward. In moving once people find a company they liked they often stick with them all the time. That loyalty in addition to our corporate accounts allowed me to have many repeat customers. Not only would they call our company again and again, but they would also ask for drivers by name, I have met many people over and over again in my career.

We had some great fun in those days and really learned a lot about business and life while I worked the next couple of years with that agent. Sometimes you don't realize how much you learn on the job training. I started to get more regional moves out of town that helped me with my business skills. I had acquired a steady helper at the company who would be there for all moves. His name was Rupert and we became fast friends outside of work as well. As a team we became such good movers that very rarely did we need to take a third person with us on moves. Moving is like a dance and is more technique than muscle. You need to learn how to lift using the least amount of energy using simple equipment like straps. With properly used straps on a washing machine you can walk forever with the machine because the weight is distributed properly. Experienced movers know this making them able to carry things that are heavier farther.

I would learn to negotiate with Rupert for out of town moves. The thing about moving is that you begin to work as if you are owner operator even if you don't own the truck. Regional and highway work is paid on percentage of the move, of course if you own the truck your percentage is higher, but even company owned equipment is dispatched the same way. So if I have a move going from Toronto to Montreal I would get a certain percentage of the revenue. I didn't have to pay for the truck, but I did have to pay fuel and help if needed and expenses.

These became quite popular and of course all drivers were hoping to get this type of work. Our agency did quite a bit if regional work so I did quite well as a mover. Having a partner like Rupert made it easy for me to negotiate because we could calculate exactly how long the move took. Often we would drive there and back in the same day to avoid hotels. I would pay all meals and a day rate, something I learned at my last place of employment. I became my own little owner operator. A business model that I would adopt for the rest of my career and life to be exact, more on that in later chapters. Soon after starting at the North American agent I began to get the itch to move up from a "D" license. I had been there a couple of years and began to let them know I was ready to move on to larger vehicles.

The truck they had for a tractor trailer was and old GMC gas single axle gas tractor. I had become friends with Andre, the driver of the truck and asked if he would teach me to drive it. There were very few schools in those days and the ones out there cost way too much money for me. I was lucky that the company was situated in a small commercial area so on Sundays I would come in and practice driving the truck. I would back into docks in the area, no one was open and the area was considered private property so I didn't have to worry as long as I didn't hit anything. That went on for months until I felt confident about driving and taking the test. Whenever I was with Andre he would let me drive and since I was the only other one besides Andre who knew how to drive the truck there were a few times when he was sick and I was sent out on my own to handle a move. After a few of those I decided I better get in there and get the license and I did. One of the best things you can do for yourself is to keep learning and many of the other drivers at the agent had the same opportunity as I did, but they didn't ask. By achieving my class "A" license I secured my future again, when work got slow, they weren't firing the guys with the license, they were firing the guys without. It always amazes me that people stop in their career path and just settle for the level they are at. Why not secure your future even farther and open up more opportunities. Getting the license moved me to the top of the totem pole at the company as far as drivers go.

When you're the class "A" driver you are the only one that can drive every piece of equipment in the yard, making you valuable, I tell people all the time do not settle for a "D" license even if you only want to drive a straight truck, keep your options open. As I began to drive larger equipment even more opportunity started coming my way in the way of more highway trips. Not necessarily with the tractor trailer because that was Andre's unit but being the second driver on the list I was at the top when these opportunities became available. I had surpassed the driver who had been there for many years before me, but because he didn't upgrade himself he actually ended up on the list behind me for many opportunities. He got so mad that he wouldn't talk to me and when he saw I was still getting the opportunities for out of town moves he eventually sulked and quit. What did that do for me but gave me even more moves in the regional area allowing me to make even more money. Thank you! If you insist on staying at a certain level don't be surprised when a someone comes and blows by you like the wind, it will happen. Life is a competition of sorts, don't treat people unfairly, but keeping your options open with good training is just smart thinking.

I wasn't planning on going into business for myself at that time but we had an owner operator with a straight truck that used to travel Toronto to the East Coast and seemed to do pretty well. He worked for a sister agent of ours and I was amazed that he could make money with such a small truck. Many of the owner operators at that time had tractor units. He said that his truck was perfect because he could load one load and go leaving his down time to a minimum while owner operators of larger trucks had to wait for three or four shipments to make it worthwhile to roll down the road. I was intrigued that he owned his own truck, but didn't know enough about trucking to know how to enter the system, but that would change. Andre and I had become good friends and I applaud him to this day for helping me start my trucking career. Not only did he help me get my license, but helped me get my US experience. Andre's dad also worked for our van lines agent and was the U.S. broker. He would run Toronto to Florida most of the time, but all his loads were US bound. We also had a Canadian owner operator, but every so often Andre would take a load for his Dad if there was a conflict in the schedule. Especially in the winter when things were slow at our agent. Andre asked if I would like to join him for a run to Cleveland Ohio, well it may as well been Florida, I was so excited to go.

This would be the first time out of the country trucking and I had no idea what to expect. I followed Andre like a lost puppy who was just happy to be brought along in the International tractor that sat much higher than the little GMC we drive around the city. We arrived at customs to find we had a seven hour wait while they tore the shipment apart. Welcome to my first dealing with US Customs. Most people would have turned away at that point. I talk with many people who went into trucking and had a bad experience and they say they are never going back there again. If you want to make money in this business realize that not everyone is out to get you and suck it up. If I had turned around at that point I would have missed out on a thirty year career. Shortly after our Cleveland dilemma Andre invited me on another trip. This trip was particularly fun for me because he let me drive the truck. I remember our destination was Blue Grass Iowa and I still consider it the coldest place on the planet.

I am sure it isn't but when we arrived there it seemed like minus 20, the place was cold and dark, and had one street light. To me there was no way that someone was moving to a place that cold and planning on living there. We were only there overnight, delivered and headed back, but I still remember the darkness of that town. That trip did something for us however, it got us talking. Andre and I got along very well and worked well together. We began to think of possibilities owning our own truck and how we should start a business together. We realized we both liked the moving business, were getting older at the ripe age of twenty, and were starting to get a little bored moving people around the city. We decided that a partnership would be the best for both of us as we both could drive, both could move, and both would have a stake in the operation. There was one problem, we were two twenty somethings with no money, no truck, nothing more than a want. What did we have going for us? We went back to our lives working for the van lines as we pondered what could have been, but in business as many entrepreneurs would know that once that seed has been opened it is hard to put it back in the shell. The shell was definitely broken.

You should have asked advice first!

Since Andre and I worked for the same agent our paths would cross before and after work not to mention the occasional party on a Saturday night. Every time we were in company our conversation would head back towards the venture of owning a truck. We felt we had it down although we would learn that wasn't so. After about six months of bantering about the project I received a call from Andre. He had been working on his Dad in the background and had managed to get his father to lend us ten thousand dollars to buy a truck. He even had a truck picked out. It turns out a friend of his that worked for another Atlas Van Lines agent in Georgetown Ontario had a team operation that was getting out of the business. They had an old W900 tractor that had been customized for a double bunk and it was going for ten thousand dollars. Andre and I met with his dad and came to an agreement, The ten thousand dollars was Andre's investment into the company and I would put up the operating capital once we got rolling. Neither of us would take a pay cheque other than enough to cover our basic living expenses. Heck we were going to be rich anyway so it was just a matter of time, right! Needless to say Salt and Pepper Trucking was born, that's right, that's what we called it. The reason was simple, Andre was white and I was brown or black if you must say it. Even though I am not deep brown in those days I might as well been called "Negro" and took much ribbing for it from school right into the ripe old age of thirty years old. Today people don't even see my colour, but back then it was a big thing. I learned to laugh it off which helped me be more respected in a weird way. We registered the company as such and I signed a partnership agreement between us with my Dad's assistance. I never forget the first time I saw the truck we bought.

Ten thousand dollars seemed like a lot of money for the truck we bought, it was a cabover, diesel, that had a unique sleeper conversion. A hole had been cut in the top of the sleeper roof and a nose cone for a trailer had been attached to the top, so the second sleeper was really the roof of the truck. A mattress had been put up there and believe it or not the old driver Randy made his wife sleep up there.

Now Randy had to weigh around four hundred pounds and his wife was big as well. I couldn't imagine either of them sleeping up there but they did. We had some work to do which was not well thought out. The truck needed to be stripped of the old running stickers, those were the days when the truck was covered in State Authority stickers. The truck needed repainting, so while we were waiting for our authorities to go through and name changes we started working on the truck. Now we bought the truck in November, we had quit North American and moved to the Atlas Agent. The agent was good to us and tried to give us local work to keep income coming in while we set up the truck, but things seemed to take forever. Stripping the truck meant heating stickers up with a hair dryer, and we borrowed enough money from Andre's dad only for the paint job which was plain white. We finally got everything together after two months working outside and were ready to go. Now if you ever decide to start a business, timing is everything and in those days moving came to a crawl in November until spring. We were ready to go the beginning of January. Most people are shutting their trucks down for the winter.

This trailer cone was the supposed custom sleeper, yeah right!

We finally got a load at the end of January, it had been a really slow winter and we needed some cash. Our first load was moving an executive from Georgetown Ontario to Ft. Lauderdale Florida. We were excited, not only did we get a decent load, but going to a warmer climate, I still had visions of Blue Grass Iowa in my mind. The trip went well with Andre guiding me as I learned to handle our new truck. We did well until we hit the scale just south of Jacksonville Florida. We got pulled into an inspection and found we didn't have some permit we needed. We also didn't have the three hundred dollars they were asking for in cash. I was using my credit card for fuel and the operation budget was almost tapped out, when a familiar truck came around. Andre's Dad happened to pull through the scale while we were there helping us with some much needed cash. We arrived in FT. Lauderdale and spent the night parked across from the beach in an empty parking lot. I drew the short straw so had to sleep in the make shift sleeper. I was comfortable until the sun came up. Fibreglass has a way of generating heat like I have never seen before. I woke up at five in the morning dripping of sweat as the sun turned our truck into a steam bath. Nothing however beat the sight of Andre shaving and showering at the beach showers across the road. Passersby would stop to check out his shaving program. We delivered the load and found that while we had a good idea of saving money we forgot that two healthy boys like to eat and drink. To save money we stayed in the truck with the exception of one night when Andre's Father was heading back home empty and gave us his hotel room. You can only spend so much time in a truck so we would hit the bars at night and almost started a bar brawl when a drunk in the bar started to become racial towards me at the all night bar at three in the morning. They got him out before we had to do any fighting. After two weeks as if we were on vacation we started to head back to Canada, empty. The trick we later found out was to run south, wait two days and if no load came in you returned home empty cutting your losses. We spent much needed money those two weeks. Andre and I continued on for another year and half but just weren't making it. My debt was getting higher and higher and it came to a point that the partnership wasn't going to work for the long term.

After two years I decided to get out of the business. Andre paid me out and kept going with the truck for a short time later until he eventually sold it himself. I was able to get my position back at the North American agent for a couple of more years before deciding to move over to the freight side of the industry. My first lesson in business had been a hard one especially at the age of twenty-two, but one I would never forget.

I learned a lot about business, being properly funded, and how to manage a working partnership. I realized that I need to move into something more structured where work wouldn't come to a crawl in the winter and I could keep a pay cheque coming in steadily. Although I had five years experience in the industry I would learn that I had to start at the bottom of the pile again, but in my mind freight was the way to go.

Summary

Using your passion will take you to new heights in your career and business, but you have to be watching out for the best path or the next step. Settling for your current place won't make you money in the long run you need to keep moving and learning. Even if the step up doesn't work out you have a new experience to add to your belt.

Customer Service is paramount in any industry but especially when dealing with the public. The training has never let me down to this very day and I feel should be the first thing taught in the truck driver's tool box. If you don't care either will your customers and no matter what they control the income. Learn good customer service skills and you will extend your career for a long time.

Summary Continued.......

If you do decide to follow your entrepreneurial spirit make sure you do your homework. At the time we thought having an agreement in place and our experience we were ready to go. A solid business plan would have shown us otherwise which we later found out. We got out relatively unscathed but things could have been worse. We were both young enough to recover, however I spent many years afterward trying to get my finances back in order. Often we think of the benefits of an operation but not the negative side. That negative side is the side that will bring your operation to a halt. Be properly funded and realize the money won't come rolling in just because you're in business. I never regretted the experience and learned more than I would have ever learned without it. Never regret the lessons in your life.

In trucking customer service is paramount to getting new business however most drivers miss the boat on this and wonder why they don't make more money than they do.

Chapter 2
Owning Your Position

The goal to steady money was the driving force for the change. I enjoyed the moving industry and it taught me a lot about dealing with people both colleagues and customers, but I was young and needed something I could rely on all year long. Many of the owner operators in the moving industry were starting to haul computer and trade show equipment around in the winter, however computers were still a dream back then so it was very scarce work if you could find it at all. Freight however was always flowing, but getting into this side of the industry proved a little harder than the moving side.

The first freight or cartage company I ran for was Queensway Cartage. The owner Keith had been a former over the road driver and with his wife working in the office had decided to make a go of having their own trucking company. Keith was a likable guy and I enjoyed working at the company, but it was not a company that you would have a career with. We were paid ten dollars an hour which was average back then and I was hired for a contract to deliver groceries to the Dominion stores around Ontario. I was to work every evening, but that never lasted very long. I think I delivered for them for a month before the contract went dry and the work stopped. They were strict on who worked there and only overflow was given to outside carriers. So, many nights I would show up and sit around waiting for a load and nothing would happen. Finally the company got some other contracts and day work showed up.

The company only had two tractor trailers and an owner operator from Buffalo would come and help out, I am not sure where he fit in to the whole mix, but I learned many lessons from working at Queensway. I drove a tractor where every time I turned, the drive axles would shift to the right or left. I kept asking for repairs but nothing was ever done. Once in a blue moon a cheque would bounce and I would be told some sob story. The trailers were crap and I used to dream about one day having a nice truck to drive. Whenever I saw trucks passing me that had chrome on them and they had not been taken care of, it would drive me crazy and I vowed that I would never let my truck go like that. Even the truck I was driving I tried to paint the wheels on my own dime one day and kept the junk heap as clean as I could.

Even when they were going out of business I didn't see it coming, the work was drying up; we were told that it wouldn't be long before the doors close. The owners were very nice and they told me they would pay me to the end, so the last week they asked me to take Keith's car and drive around and pick up cheques. The other driver had found another job already and I should have been out pounding the pavement but didn't really know where to go. So I drove around picking up cheques for the owner. At the end of the week I was given a cheque that of course bounced. I was never able to get hold of the owner after that and at that point I changed the way I did business as a driver. In my book out on the market "Running By The Mile" I talk about how just because someone has experience in the industry doesn't make them business savvy. I should have learned many of these lessons already from the moving side with my own truck but I wasn't able to see the money and books of the company.

You can play basketball with this cheque

Watching the signs is a good way of protecting your job. If the company is losing contracts on a regular basis, maintenance isn't being done, or pay cheques are bouncing get the hell out of there.

As I didn't hit the pavement when I should have and was limited not having a car to get around I decided to start working for a few agencies. I was told there was good money there. So I would phone up a couple of agents during the day and hope they had work. A few would hire you once but to get loads on a regular basis you had to buy the dispatch a bottle so I learned to stay away from those. A few others gave me work but you would spend all day calling them and then they would want you there in an hour. I found it too up and down and very stressful. So I began seriously looking for a job with a decent company.

Working for the companies like Queensway which by the way is different from Queensway Tank Lines today, taught me some great lessons. I would only work for companies that were stable financially, I would only drive well maintained equipment, and I would treat all equipment as if it was my own. These three items have shaped my career for the rest of my life and still work for me today. These lessons made me strive for better which in turn made me more money. It was the start of Outridge University as I called it, always strive for the best.

I was now hitting the streets to find work realizing I would never work well with a temporary agency. I didn't have a car, only a bicycle so I began to ride around filling out applications at any companies I thought looked like a place I would want to work. As much as Queensway was a bad job it did help me in the way of experience even if it was NOT to do. I had hauled some loads of groceries, and was comfortable with city pick up and deliveries so I stuck with finding city work at this point. I did my best to follow the rules I had set out above. Of course I couldn't tell if companies were financially stable, but if they had been around for a while that was the best I could ask for. Before applying to the company I would ride around back and take a look at their trucks, if I didn't like the oldest truck in the yard then I didn't apply. As a new driver you will get the oldest piece of equipment that is in the yard until you prove yourself. Assume that unless that truck is used solely as a yard truck, it will be the new person's truck. The equipment had to be mechanically sound and if they had a garage on the property even better. I was not getting into another situation like Queensway, so I applied to a number of companies and was able to get on with a city company which is now Manitoulin Transport.

I was hired to work in the pickup and delivery section. There was around ten of us and we all drove single axle International tractors and pup trailers. The work was hourly, and I had a steady area which was Scarborough, south of the 401 as my customer base. We would deliver in the morning and pickup in the afternoon for around a nine hour day. I was able to ride my bike to work and in the winter I would pay for a fellow driver to pick me up. I then began to apply my last rule of running the truck as if I owned it. Something my fellow drivers never seemed to figure out. The trucks were very basic without even a radio except for the company radio tuned into dispatch. When they got a call they would call you with the details and you would go and pickup the freight. I installed a radio for music, only AM back then so I could enjoy the day. I wiped off my truck every morning so that it looked like it had just been washed and even brought in my own can of paint to paint the wheels back to white. Many of the other drivers wondered why I went to the trouble of wiping down my truck, it's not like they had chrome on them or were show trucks of any kind, just basic single axle Internationals.

When the company did buy new equipment, who do you think got it? I remember they bought a new Mack single axle and presented it to me. I was the only one taking care of their equipment, as the saying goes, "They will show you how much they care when you show how much you care." Drivers often don't want to take the initiative of making the first step and working not knowing if a reward is around the corner. I have found if you always take the first step it will come back to you, remember "What goes around comes around!" I have lived by that motto my whole life and it has always come through.

Many of our customers were the same for both deliveries and pickups and we had regular customers that we picked up at every day, so I kept a little black book with all my regulars numbers. For regular customers we were to drive around each day and see if they had anything to ship. I decided to call the regulars from another customer's phone to ask if they had anything to ship, many times they didn't so it saved me driving over to their location. This would give me a longer lunch or time to clean the truck. Good time management is paramount in the transportation industry and city pickups are no exception. Working smart always trumps working hard.

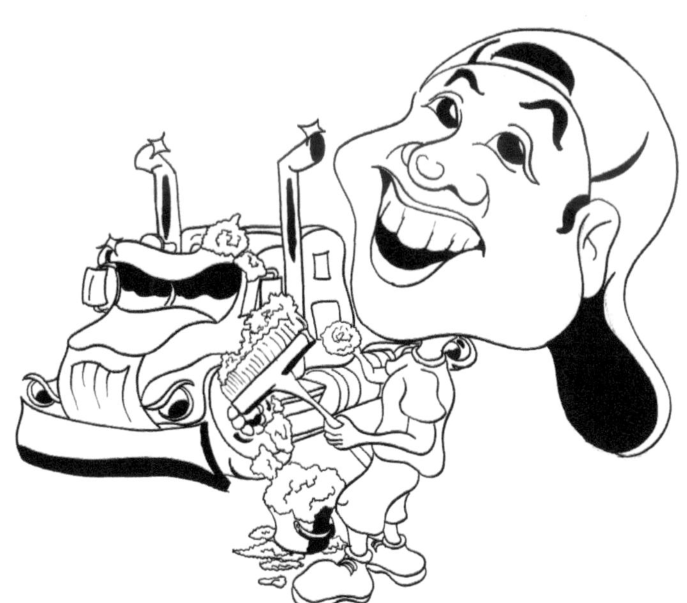

Professionalism is a choice!

My counterpart on the North side of the 401 was totally opposite to me. He was filthy! He would eat crap all day and throw it on the floor of his truck, washing and showering was an option, and his truck was so bad no one else would drive it. It was the only time I had ever refused work was the day I was asked to drive his truck. He used to haul portable toilets on weekends to make extra money, need I say more? I would get a call from dispatch almost every day at four o'clock in the afternoon to go help this driver because he was falling behind on his pickups and the customers were closing. Talk about dogging it! Back in those days most drivers only made ten dollars an hour so everyone was looking for a way to make extra money.

Those were the days of cashing our cheques at the strip joint. It was fun but we all needed more money to live. Keeping your nose clean was the best way to get more work. We all had a couple of jobs that didn't pay very much. We worked Monday to Friday so I began to pick up extra shifts before and after my shift. I would come in at five in the afternoon from my run and help the shipping team load the trucks for up north until around 6:30pm giving me extra time. I would also come in at 5:00 in the morning and unload and load the city deliveries. Making the best of wasted time is the best way to make money. All the drivers would come in for 8:00am and go directly to break while the highway trailers were being unloaded. They would have their sticky buns and coffee and roll out around 9:00am for their deliveries. Because I was loading them I didn't leave until 10:00am and still had to help the other guys.

I was able to get in a twelve hour day instead of an eight hour day and two of those hours were overtime so I was making good money compared to the rest. However I was looking for more, as much as I enjoyed the city I was looking to get back on the highway.

I began making calls but kept getting the same answer, I wasn't old enough. Back then you had to be 25 to be properly insured, but there is always a way. Many people give up on their careers because they have been told "no" but there is always a way around a problem. One of my regular pickups was a magazine distributor. They had a dozen of their own trucks not in great condition but they were highway tractors. They ran regional and had weekend runs within Ontario. I was talking with the shipper and managed to get hired as a temporary employee taking loads to Barrie and Collingwood on weekends. It didn't pay much but it was extra work on top of the fifty to sixty hours I was working during the week. There were no log books in Canada back then so that wasn't a problem. The trucks were terrible with boot marks on the roof of the sleeper, no way was I sleeping in there, but I just focused on the money. That gave me the gateway to getting into the magazine business. I was getting bored with city work and wanted to branch out.

At a family gathering I got talking to my wife's uncle who used to haul cars. As a birthday present one day I polished his whole truck while he slept and we got along well at family functions, so one day he made a call to a terminal manager he knew after I was telling him I wanted to get out on the highway. The next week I had an interview and was giving my notice a week after that. The company was sad to see me go and I too enjoyed working there but you can't get stuck in your growth. There is a time when you have to move on and this was my time. It had been two years and I was tired. I see so many drivers stick it out in one place because they are afraid of change and when they get the gumption to move, it is too late. Don't do that to yourself, you'll regret it later. Early in my career I found I was moving every two years. It was no grand strategic plan; I just seemed to be ready to move on after that. That's because you're growing and ready to move on to better and bigger things. This was my time to move up again, this time to the big rigs.

Summary

If I've learned anything I've learned to play by my own rules. That first company taught me quite a bit about what I don't want for my life and career. This is where most new drivers make mistakes; they go for any company that will hire them to get experience. I understand that I did the same thing, but don't feel you have to stay there forever. Always be striving for a better place to work. Keep an eye on the operation of your workplace, they won't let you see the books, but if they begin refusing to fix equipment, accounts seem to come and go, or even worse your pay cheque bounces, get the hell out of there. Those are telltale signs a business is in trouble.

Own your position, and that starts at the very beginning. Do your homework on a company; check out their equipment, even the old stuff because that is what you will be driving in the beginning. Ask questions and don't be afraid to dive in and take on extra duties. When I left the city operation they thought they were losing two men. Don't be afraid to own your position by taking care of the equipment as if you own it. If you only gain one idea from this book I would say that would be the biggest thing you could take away, treat the equipment as though you had to pay for it. Keep it clean and while you don't need to buy paint and paint things yourself keeping a unit that looks good to customers will help you and your career down the road.

Keep looking for opportunities to move forward in your career. There is nothing worse than someone who should have moved on, decided not to, and then turns negative about the industry. They are like a cancer growing in the company. Every career has a beginning where you are in learning mode, and then you will reach your comfort level when you work for a decent company and are successful in what you do. At that point if you don't learn new skills or move up the ladder you will eventually start to go down in your career, and many times without even knowing it. That is where the cancer starts and things will be a tough road ahead. I have seen this countless times and as far as I am concerned when it happens, those people should either leave the industry or stop talking to people because they aren't helping. I met one of those early on and if I had listened to him I would still be pumping gas. Don't let that happen to you, always be on upward swing.

I see so many drivers stick it out in one place because they are afraid of change and when they get the gumption to move, it is too late.

Chapter 3

Finding Your Dream Job

The phone call to the magazine carrier was a great step in my career. I was given an opportunity that would make a real difference in my life. I got the job of driving for a private carrier called Printer's Transport. The company hauled magazines of all sorts and is what I considered to be my dream job. We had a fleet of twelve or thirteen trucks; the Dispatcher and Terminal Manager had both driven before and were in fact married. They were great people and made the place a fun place to work. It was like working with one big happy family. They ran the U.S and Canada, had decent equipment, and only ran the Midwest and Southern States. It was a dream job.! We had one driver located in Buffalo New York and the others including myself were based in Oakville Ontario. Our runs were to steady customers and locations so we knew exactly where we were going at all times.

I loved that job and like the ones before I acted as if I owned that equipment. No matter how old the equipment they gave I would polish it up as if it was brand new. As people moved into other positions or some drivers at the top didn't get their way and would quit I would move into a nicer truck. I loved the people, at the time the wages were at the top end and we got paid for everything we did. Yes, there was some work involved, schedules were very important and many of the loads were still loaded on the floor so hand bombing was part of the job; however there were still plenty of positives that made the job great. Much of it was to do with the people and people can make or break and organization. Our dispatch was a girl named Brenda and in those days women weren't very prominent in the industry. Not only that but she was good, she knew her stuff, was very organized, but the best part was she would back you up. I never forgot the time that a customer tried to accuse the drivers of tardiness or something like that and she got on that phone and made them aware of how wrong they were and where their facts went wrong. I would never forget that and this is something that I don't see in many transport companies today. Many times the drivers are blaming the dispatchers, the dispatchers are blaming the drivers, and everyone is blaming management. If people owned their position instead of trying to get out of everything the world would be a better place, however that's not the case.

On Friday afternoons we would all meet after work and it really helped us bond and learn what people are like outside of work. They created a team environment that started from the top and worked down. The owners of the business were amazing people themselves and that flowed down through the rest of the team, even people in the warehouse. It was one of the best times of my life in trucking, so much so that it didn't even feel like work. It was fun to come to work, the runs were good, the people were great, and it was certainly my dream job.

Dreams can turn to nightmares however, I had been at the company for a few years and was really in my prime when the meeting came. We were called one Saturday to our boss's home for a meeting to discuss the future of our positions. It turns out that the company was being sold and they were cutting some positions to make things attractive to new buyers. I had been at the bottom of the list along with a friend named Tommy that started about the same time I did. We were devastated as they rolled out the news saying 20% of the drivers would be let go, although we weren't union employees I was at the bottom and knew I would be let go. I have never seen a group enjoy their positions so much that they tried to bargain down by sharing income. As a group we asked questions such as if we all gave back a few cents per mile could we keep everyone on? Was there anything we could do to make sure people stayed on part-time, but nothing worked? The decisions were already made and even worse our bosses were losing their jobs as well. I physically felt sick inside, it was the first time I had ever been laid off and to have it with a job that at that time of my life was my dream job was unbelievable. My career had finally started going in the right direction in my eyes and this was an intense blow. As much as I liked the runs, the equipment, and the freedom to be the person I wanted to be, you have to move on. We got the official notice and three drivers from the bottom lost their jobs. The Terminal Manager lost his job; however they kept his wife Brenda in dispatch, very smart move. The real joy of that job was the people and I thought I would never work for a company like that ever again.

My former Terminal Manager was moving on and had found some other opportunities and asked if I was interested. One place was Pizza Pizza which was just beginning with their own fleet at the time which didn't pan out and my boss ended up at a place named Samson's Trucking. I was hesitant to go but thought following my old boss Gary would be a good move. He and I both were a little surprised at the state of the company, but Gary was hired to bring the company up to speed. It moved me to the top of the list, but a short list doesn't give you much of a boost.

I have been talking about finding your dream job and whether you even think there is one. I am sure you have also heard that line, "You won't know how good you had it until it's gone!" Well I was about to enter into that period of my life. It almost seemed like the trucking company was a write off for other businesses and not the main focus. There were thirteen trucks including the owner operators and they were a mess. The owner had given Gary free rein to clean things up and that meant spending some money on much needed equipment. Gary brought one piece from the past, the old beloved Western Star from Printer's Transport where we worked previously. The truck had been Gary's workhorse and was given to only certain individuals. It was assigned to me because he knew it would be taken care of. We worked like that for a year before letting it go and buying brand new equipment across the board. Unfortunately new trucks do not make a good company. The top owner operator was the boss's son that knew nothing about trucking but thought he did. He was your typical star struck driver that only ran California. He would sit if there was no load for the West meanwhile he was so behind on his payments his own father was threatening to throw him out of the truck. We had another driver who was very nice but because he couldn't speak English very well he would run out West and have a heck of a time coming home, he would be stuck out there for weeks. Out of the thirteen people on the team four of them could be trusted with a load and get it there on time. Our dispatcher was a nice girl who didn't really know trucking but had a great phone voice. She would get flustered very often and not know where things were. I don't know how many times she lost my paperwork. I would sit in and dispatch for her when she was on vacation, so it gave me some experience there. It also gave me the bird's eye view of how different drivers operate.

We had another guy that didn't shower and you couldn't stand next to him in the office. It got to the point that I learned what I didn't want for a company and I also learned a very hard lesson, how to protect my money.

Many drivers go through this and never learn how to protect themselves. Administration staff may lose a trip envelope, our maybe a receipt goes missing and the driver will attempt to battle it out with nothing to show to back them up, but admit they have paid it. If the driver or company is bad with paperwork this can begin to happen on a regular basis. This was starting to happen to me, but I am a quick learner and saw that it wasn't me not handing things in, but the office having bad paper management. When this happened I started completing my paperwork at the office in front of the dispatcher, I would photocopy my trip envelope and then hand it to the clerk. I would file my copy in my truck or car and whenever there was a missed envelope I would produce my copy. As soon as I did that they knew they had their copy in the office. Many times they would borrow mine in order to pay me. I kept that going for most of my driving career and after that never had a problem getting paid. Take your money into your own hands and back up your stuff, you work hard for your money. It amazes me that people will rely on someone else to control their schedule of payments. By photocopying the paperwork in front of them it showed them that I am watching things from my side and they had better smarten up on their side. Hopefully, you won't have to work for bad companies but I think we all do at one time or another. Whether it is a pay issue or something else such as vacation time, be ready to set yourself apart from the rest and act as if the company is your customer.

"We'll have to pay him now!"

After another year of this fiasco I decided it was time to part ways. I was sorry to leave Gary, he was a great boss, but he too was ready to move on and had begun to look for other opportunities. I just couldn't see me going far with that company and I was looking for a place to call home. It was suggested that I try a little company in Burlington that was hot at the time and growing like a weed. It would be a suggestion that would stay with me the rest of my career.

Summary

Dream jobs don't come along very often and when they do if you are not on the top of your game you can miss them. Some of the best companies to work for are private carriers and Printer's Transport was the first one for me. Taking ownership of your equipment is a great way to move up and prove yourself and that is something you will have to do in good company to stay on. Working hard from the beginning will give you a name that people can trust and this will help your career, they will want to take you with them up the ladder, that may or may not be very beneficial however, but don't be afraid to try opportunities.

Many drivers have been with companies so long they don't understand when they have a good thing going. Usually that is a sign they have been at the company too long or have forgotten the roots that got them started in the business. Working for bad companies can help you to decide the kind of carriers you would like to work for.

If you have proven yourself don't be afraid to leave the nest and go for something new, it may be the best thing that ever happened to your career. Knowing what you "don't want" will help you know what you want, trust me! Protect yourself, you are working hard for your pay cheque, if you are having trouble getting paid, or being reimbursed for company purchases photocopy everything. Pretend you are your own company and the trucking company is your customer. That trip envelope is your invoice, lose that and you don't get paid. I don't know about you but I like to get paid. Many people try to fight without backing themselves up. Having a hard copy is one way of doing that and the boss will start to respect you for taking the initiative to making sure things are handed in timely. Don't let other people control your money. You've worked hard for it!

Working hard from the beginning will give you a name that people can trust and this will help your career!

Chapter 4
Balancing Family and Work

You'll come to a point in your life where you have proven yourself enough that the interviews get easier and your resume looks better. I was at the nine year mark of my career; I had worked for good and bad companies, and had a good name in the industry from all my previous employers. I began working at a company in Burlington Ontario at the end of 1988 and felt as though I was at home. The company hauled a variety of freight, had some good contracts, and fun people to work with. The equipment was excellent with big Peterbilts, extra-long Freightliners, and fancy chrome; everything was right down my alley. The company was also known for being a money maker. It wasn't so much that they paid more than everyone else however, they were on the leading edge of the pay scale, but that they paid for everything.

If you are looking to make money in transportation, don't just look at the company mileage rate, look at things such as, do they pay actual miles, or PC miles? Do they pay for drops and pickups; do they pay for border crossings? It is the little things that make you money. I remember a load I took to Miami Florida that was a multi drop load with six deliveries and a straight load back. As a driver I made around $1500.00 for that load alone. I took a similar load the next time with a straight load each way and only made around $800.00. Since I had always hauled multi-drop loads in the past I enjoyed that system where others like the straight loads. That's because I would make money on the border crossings, and the deliveries almost doubling the income.

Be smart when trucking and you will make more money. I think the reason I felt so at home is that my system of owning your position really got noticed at this company. All the trucks were nicely decked out, some more than others, however not everyone kept them that way. So if you treated the truck like your own and put in the extra effort to keep it looking good you got noticed because the owners were into that. Many tried to say I was sucking up, but I had always been that way. Never change because of the pressure of others. When you're happy at your job it will make a big difference in your pay and it did to mine. I went everywhere they sent me and loved it, there was only two rules that I set out, I would not sleep in New York City if a load wasn't ready, and I had no interest in running the West Coast unless absolutely necessary. Those are the only two stipulations I had and have always lived by. With a yard of around forty trucks all chromed out there were enough drivers wanting the miles of the West Coast so let them go. As much as I loved my job I also wanted to be home regularly and that meant weekly if possible. My whole time there I was never asked to go out west, and my pay showed I had made the right choice.

Two things drove me to stay homeward bound, California was straight loads much of the time so you had miles but none of the other income from side deliveries or border crossings. While a driver is driving to California he is spending four days going one way just driving. If I ran New Jersey even with one delivery each way that would pay me an extra $200 above my mileage income and usually it was more than that. California would take two weeks to complete, in that period I would have done five round trips to the East Coast, at $200 per trip I would have made close to a $1000 more than my friend running the West Coast if the mileage was even. Running longer does not necessarily make you more money, plus you get the added benefit of seeing your family on the weekends, "Working smart always out works working hard". I was dedicated to my truck and rose up the ranks quickly, rising up the ranks in a transport company doesn't mean more pay, but can raise your income. When you are promoted inside a company, many times that means better runs, better equipment, and choice of travel areas. I had all of that during my time there. They kept giving me a better truck each year, my runs got longer and longer depending on where I wanted to go.

The real money was in the East Coast but for those of you running there on a regular basis you know that it can take the life out of you. Constant traffic, tolls, congested streets, rude people, bad areas and so forth can make you crazy after a while. The company was smart, they had six of us that would run that area until the cows come home and not blink an eye. We knew the areas like clockwork and could get in and out of the city in no time. That was even stressful to us so once a month we would usually be sent in a different direction. My favourite runs were Florida or Texas with Houston being the overall winner. Why Houston you ask? Texas is every truck drivers dream run. To get to Houston it would take you around thirty hours which is a two day run one way. You would spend a day or so in the area delivering and picking up another load and then you had a two day drive back home. It gave you good miles; it was easy driving with warm weather, little mountains, and large highways. You could easily avoid major cities and it would make for a relaxing week. Miami was much the same. This would give us a break of the traffic of the East Coast so it was much appreciated. The real secret of running and making money however is not so much the area you run, but how you run with good time management always winning and if you want to make true money in trucking, time management had better become your friend.

I pride myself on being on time and always have. I am not sure why because not only in school was I late, but would sometimes not even attend. In the work world however the good work ethic instilled by my parents taught me not to be late on the job and in transportation that is even more important. When I was hauling magazines, we had delivery appointments with the different distributors and they expected you around the same time each week. At this company they had an underlying rule that you must deliver between seven and nine each morning unless another time had been arranged. So if you left Toronto on Monday afternoon for New Jersey you were expected to deliver between seven and nine Tuesday morning. If you were leaving for Florida on Monday you would be expected to deliver in Miami between seven and nine Wednesday morning and so on. This was normal practice for the whole fleet. The part I missed when I started with the company is that it was only a rule for outbound loads, but I didn't know that. I thought we had to deliver the same time both ways.

So if I delivered in New Jersey on Tuesday morning, I would deliver in Toronto, Wednesday morning, New York Thursday morning, and so on. No wonder I made so much money, always listen to the whole set of rules. I can't complain however as I always made good money and that same dedication started me on dedicated runs that would solidify my position at the company. I enjoyed working the way I did and started to feel as though I had made a home.

Although the team gave me a hard time due to my colour (most people don't consider me black but I am to a point) I accepted a lot of kidding around from the mechanics and other drivers. One of the biggest things they would say is the company sent me to New Jersey because of the colour of my skin. My reply to them was at least I would come back! I found in school when I was growing up that you can either fight the world or find a way to live in it. My way of living in it was to fight them back with a better joke and it worked. Even though they were teasing me they were accepting me at the same time, because I could take that joke. Teamed with my dedication to the equipment and hard work ethic many of those people are still my friends to this day. I was even getting crap from those that thought I was brown nosing by washing my truck all the time and getting attention that way, however I had dealt with that kind before and ignoring them seemed to be the best way to deal with them. There is a small group in every company that thinks the same way and the group you associate with will determine the way you think. I chose to hang out with the chrome junkies that kept their trucks immaculate and so I became accepted in that group. I still talked to the other guys it's just their whining would get old after a while. So even with all the kidding the place was home. I saw a nice long career with the company and was enjoying myself immensely when one weekend I found out some important information; it came at me like a news flash.

My wife informed me that we were pregnant. Being a trucker in love with his truck I asked her how long and she informed me four weeks. I counted back four weeks and said it can't be I was in Kentucky. Guys can be so naive; however it was true and we're going to have a baby in June of 89. The pregnancy didn't bother me at all, I just kept trucking, my wife had a good support network in her family, and so I kept going down the road.

I don't even think I told the boss until it was closer to the date and I would need a few days off. In trucking if the wheels aren't turning you aren't earning any money so things like sick days are foreign to most truck drivers. As a new person I was allowed my two weeks' vacation and that was that. As the due date came closer I informed dispatch that I would like to stay closer to home and they did their best to accommodate. The problem is that there was no city work in the operation, we had three city guys and everyone else delivered their own loads. Since I had a dedicated trailer I was responsible for picking up and delivering my own loads; so two weeks beforehand dispatch started to send me to places like Cleveland Ohio, Toledo, anywhere short that could get me home in a few hours. They started this two weeks before the due date, well didn't it turn out that my wife was two weeks late. They thought this was all a plan to keep me home. They got tired trying to keep me around and before you know it I was back to running New Jersey. I made the delivery, as it happened on a weekend.

I'm not a baby guy so while my new born son Kyle slept and ate I continued to go trucking. Now I had a baby so my first rule was to start phoning home every night. I loved kids but I also loved trucking and this would soon become a conflict. I even installed a 1-800 number so that it would be cost effective for me to phone home from wherever I was. Things went well for those first couple of years, Kyle was a good baby and slept all night and grew like a weed. Once he turned one year old I started getting this tug at my heart strings and felt the want to be home more. At this point it was only a want. One of the other drivers also had a baby around the same time but we were both chrome junkies. There was no way that our wives were going to let us run down the road all week and spend all weekend washing and cleaning the trucks so we devised a plan. We told our spouses that we would take the kids for the day so that they could have a day off and we could spend time with the kids. They bought into that like crazy and we would take the kids and meet at the shop. My friend had this little red pickup and we would take the kids toys, drive the pickup into the shop while we washed and cleaned the trucks. It was like a giant playpen for them. That's how you instill trucking in their blood, get them into the shop as soon as possible.

In 1991 my daughter came along and things really started to change. Kyle was now two, Heather was born and even though I kept running up and down the highway I wanted to be home more. I instilled the third of my own rules and decided I would either be home Friday nights before 11pm or Saturday mornings by 7am. At the time we only had one car as I was on the road each week and arriving home at 2am and asking my wife to bundle the kids up to pick me up wasn't going to happen. So I established a rule where I would try to get a full weekend home as much as possible. Sure dispatch would throw a wrench into things occasionally by announcing on Friday that I had to leave Saturday for Houston, but most of the time I was able to get home for a decent weekend. It meant no fooling around during the week however; I had to keep my foot into it. Once in a blue moon my program didn't work out so well, like the time we wanted to take the kids to a water-park. I arrived home on Saturday from a very busy week and I was exhausted, but I had kept my promise. As we arrived at the water-park I could barely keep my eyes open. My wife took the kids into the wading pool and I thought I would just catch a cat-nap under a tree. They woke me up when they were leaving six hours later, so much for family time.

Every so often on a Saturday night we invited friends over to play cards and socialize. This one couple was notorious for showing up late, if you invited them for seven they would show up at ten. One evening while playing Monopoly I was sleeping in my chair sitting up. The couple complained I was always tired when they came over, so we stopped inviting them. Problem solved! The important thing is to establish your own rules for your family. When asked to coach my son's hockey team I was reluctant to take on any duties due to my position on the road all the time, but because of my set of rules I was able to make most games and practices. You can still interact and have a life you just may have to work harder at it than most. Many folks that I talk with that are becoming new drivers feel you have to choose between family and the road, and you don't. You have to try to give them equal time. I have missed many birthdays and holidays, but the kids still survive. Instilling things like calling home every night will help them feel part of your life. I used to have the kids mark on a map where I was when I called home so that they can feel as though they are traveling with you. Make them part of your career and help them understand when you can't be there; it doesn't mean you don't love them.

Get Your Family Involved with Your Career

With two kids in the mix with activities becoming more prevalent I began to want to be home more. My son was getting older and extra activities such as hockey were something I wanted to be there to watch. My daughter didn't do as well as my son as far as sleeping during the night and took longer to settle in the early years putting more stress on the family as a whole. The thing that saved us was a beautiful couple that were the Superintendents at a building my wife lived in with her parents. They had moved closer to us and she began a daycare from her home. This has been a lifesaver for us as they treated the kids as their own. It was fine for the kids to stay overnight and they were spoiled rotten. It was helpful to me to know there was someone around to help while I was on the road. If you're on the road having a strong support system at home is very important, find people you can trust and rely on. There is enough to worry about on the road without wondering how your family is doing back home. Even though I had that support system I was still feeling that tug to be home. I began looking for ways to cut down on the highway work, but it was slim. In the end I was looking for something different, I was getting bored with long distance driving. I made two major mistakes at this point which if you are thinking this way or find yourself in a similar situation learn to ask some questions first. The two mistakes I made are that I didn't talk to anyone at the company about my options, and I made a decision based on what I saw, not what was actually available. When I was deciding to come off the road I had been with the company for around three years. I enjoyed that time and had climbed the ladder well, but was interested being around more with the kids. We had one or two city guys that from what I saw worked thirteen hour days around the city. Starting at seven in the morning until eight at night didn't seem like more home time to me, I still wouldn't see the kids. The company was a family operation from the get-go so moving into the office didn't seem like an option. Everyone was young and healthy and not going anywhere soon, so I figured I had to look elsewhere. Just at that time I was approached by my Father-in-law about starting my own business here in Ontario.

He was running for a division of Midland Transport as an owner operator and they wanted to start a new program. Instead of running the driver through Ontario to New Brunswick they decided they would set up a delivery person in Toronto.

The company had around twenty-five owner operators at this point and were running independently to the larger parent company. The drivers would bring their loads into Toronto and I was to deliver them so they could be switched back out. My father-in-law wanted to buy a second truck and lease it to me and if things went well I would buy it from him. I would run local and independently, what a dream. Exactly what I had been looking for, or was it? I quit my job with the blessings of the company after three years of employment to go work with the company. This was a brand new system so it was understandable that there would be some hiccups. For instance they couldn't work the freight routes out to end in Ontario since it was an East Coast operation so they suggested I start running like the rest of the fleet until they sorted the mess out. Needing money I went out on the highway with Charlie running team in his truck until the one he purchased was ready to go. Once I had my own truck they still didn't have things worked out so they continued to send me on what we call the East Coast triangle. Now I was supposed to be a local driver, I would leave on Saturday night for Moncton New Brunswick for Monday morning delivery. I would sit in Moncton until Wednesday either loading potatoes off Prince Edward Island or going into the U.S. with a load for New Jersey. Dispatch had this little game they played to keep you out on the road where if you lived in Toronto they sent you with a load for Montreal and vice versa. When I started working there it was one month before I got home. Was I furious! After two months of that crap I had to argue with them to send me home which they did with a line haul load. I stayed home three days and needed money so I went back on the road. They never got the program I was promised going and after six months of not being home at all I quit. I was lucky to get my position back with the company in Burlington Ontario where I had left off. Maybe it was a change I needed or maybe I was still looking for something different, but I was content to have my job back. I was refreshed and started to enjoy the road again.

The same dedication came back to my position and I was given newer equipment, the only problem was my vacation time went back to two weeks. That sixth month mistake cost me a week of vacation per year. It also taught me what I didn't want in my career.

There is one goal that can make long haul work operate as efficiently as a city job and that is the dedicated run. Usually offered to someone who has been around a while or someone dedicated to their position. We used to haul chemical back to Canada from suppliers in the United States for a chemical company. This global company had distribution centres all over the country as many of their plants made different chemicals in various locations. The company made some dangerous chemicals that awarded a higher trained team to haul it safely around the country. I had been hauling chemicals on and off to a point until now but this would be the steady deal. Three of us were asked to become part of the team for these runs, two dedicated drivers and a third as a backup. We were trained on what the chemical did, and how to best handle it in the event of a leak. Each dedicated driver would get two to three loads per week going to two or three selected plants, one on Chicago, one on North Boston, and a third in Pennsylvania. I thought this was great, dedicated work, dedicated areas, and dedicated equipment; we were like our own specialized carrier. I had no idea this work would lead to other things down the road, I was just interested in the family time.

We became so scheduled that I was able to tell my family when I would be home for a barbecue, when I was delivering, leaving, and retuning for almost the whole week. Our return loads were empty containers that had the same product so going elsewhere for back hauls were no longer an issue.
I was enjoying this new program and felt at home. With the exception of the temporary move to the East Coast carrier, I had been at the company for over four years by now, was settled into a regular family life, had new equipment every couple of years, and new exactly where I would be going each week. It sounds like a recipe for success, but there was one thing I didn't see coming, boredom.

To break up the monotony of regular runs the company would offer me a break by sending me to the East Coast or some other place I didn't usually operate in. It was a nice break and on occasion I was even able to take my son along with me. He was a hit in all the truck stops with the waitresses in his little pajamas on one trip to the East Coast, but in the end I still longed for something different. Dedicated runs are great and most like them because they offer steady income, familiar surroundings, and regular home time. I didn't realize I was a driven person until later in life but something started to happen, I got bored. The company was awesome, but I was starting to feel a tug of wanting to do more. I wanted to climb the ladder a bit but felt there was nowhere to go. I would drive down the road and I would wonder is this it, seventy hours per week, and then what? In my mind I had already decided at the start of my career I didn't want to drive until I was sixty-five. I had to keep feeling like I was moving up in the world, in my industry. I wasn't actively looking and with limited schooling my options were surely limited, the only thing I had was my good work ethic and my name. So I wrestled with this for a few years, driving along hoping something would come into my life and give me something to work towards. There is nothing worse than a person having no goals to strive for; it makes a person dead in my mind. One day in 1994 I would get a call however that changed my life to this day and I didn't even see it coming......

Summary

Balancing family and work can be very demanding on truck drivers, if you currently don't have a family take all the runs you want and get that part out of your system while you don't have any obligations to contend with. This is your time to make your name and solidify your work ethic, make yourself important to the company. Moving up in a company is what keeps you fresh, interested, and on your game. This is securing your income for the future so make the best of it. Once kids and family come along you may think that you are able to keep up the same schedule as you previously did however very few of us can. Don't make family a hindrance however, make them part of the program. Let your family be involved in your company, your operation, and your life. If they're young let them track you on the road, take them to the shop on weekends, and make them part of company picnics and the like. When they understand what you do it will make it easier to be away and they will understand the work ethic needed to be successful.

Play by your own rules, call home nightly, be available for as much time on weekends as possible and be part of their lives. I spoke to another driver waiting on a dock who said he hadn't been home in three months. When I asked if he had kids he said, "Yeah, I have thirteen of them, that's the reason I can't afford to go home." With thirteen kids I'm not sure if he can't afford to go home or doesn't want to go home either way it didn't seem to be a good family situation. Include your family in your life and dedicate yourself to them the best you can. You will be surprised how many family events and time you will be able to spend with them.

Always be moving up in your career or you will find it becomes unfulfilling. Although dedicated runs may seem like a great idea and can create some stability to a career that is often unstable it can also turn into boredom if not careful. It won't happen to everyone the same way and may not happen to some at all. You want to keep striving for better and that can be in the form of better trucks, runs, or money but keep moving along in your career or it may become the death of you. The successful people I know in transportation all enjoyed their driving careers and look back at those times as good times but in the end needed to move on to survive. Goal set your career for as long ahead as you can see, even if you don't know how you'll get there. It will develop on its own as long as there is a basic plan in place.

If you're on the road having a strong support system at home is very important, find people you can trust and rely on.

Chapter 5

Moving Up The Ladder

In late 1994 I was about to go down a new path and did, just not in the way I had expected. My dedicated run was about to be dedicated to a company. The chemical company that we did our dedicated runs for was creating a special contract and I was going to be one of the recipients of the contract and would only be working in Ontario and Quebec, there was four of us to be on this contract. This sounded good as it would afford more home time and things were set to go in a few months when I received a phone call from another driver. He asked if I was going to apply for the job of running chemicals with our customer. I didn't know anything about it, but learned afterwards that the company was starting their own fleet and interested in talking with me. I was leery at the time but went for some interviews and got the position. I think one of the reasons the interviews went so well is I didn't care if I got the job. Because I didn't know about it I didn't get all excited, so I went through the process very nonchalant making it seem a breeze.

That's one of the tricks to interviewing that many people miss, they try too hard. I know everyone wants the position but being too needy makes you look desperate. For most recruiters that gives the idea that you may be trying to hide something. A professional attitude works best for interviewing for positions. Make sure all information is filled out properly and neatly, present yourself in a professional manner, and have confidence that you are right for the position and if they don't take you not only do you have other opportunities, but they will be missing the boat and letting the best go. Keep that in your mind, don't be arrogant, but confident and you will have no trouble getting a position.

A good first impression counts!

I can tell you that it wasn't a happy process leaving the company I was with. They had treated me well and I knew this time I could never go back if things didn't work out. It had been three years since I returned from my short stint with the carrier from the East Coast and all had gone well, but this was the move I was looking for. I needed to do what was best for me, as much as it hurts you can't grow if you take chances and jump at opportunities when they arrive.

Four of us started on the same day and we felt like a small boat in a large ship. The company was a global leader of chemical production creating water treatment chemicals for industry. There was a fleet of trucks in the United States already but Canada was still an independent operation so it was like starting new. There was plenty of room to move up at this company. We started with good salaries, expense accounts, weekends off, and the freedom to do what we thought best. I call it Executive Trucking and would be the dream for many years to come. We would drive down the road and have other drivers calling us on the radio to try to get a job at the company. I did very well in this program because I had a good attitude and good customer service skills. This was no longer about trucking. The fact is that we were not even allowed to call ourselves truck drivers; we were considered and branded Customer Delivery Specialists. The change was that driving the truck was just our way of getting the chemical to the door of the customer. Our job started when we had to deliver the chemical into the tanks at the customer location without any spills or problems. We were dealing with buyers, sales reps, engineers, and maintenance workers. Before any deliveries were approved we would have to inspect the facility and with any problems apparent we could shut down the proceeding sale. This was meant as a safety issue, not a threatening way of doing business, but it put pressure on us from the sales force but they soon learned the program well and many problems were handled before we had to get involved. Attitude is very important when you have the power to shut down a million dollar sale based on your inspection, attitudes need to be kept in check!

The chemical company was a private carrier and for any of you interested in having a well-paid career as a professional driver I would suggest when you have the experience searching out those carriers of interest and applying. Most drivers can't understand the difference between a for-hire carrier and a private carrier. Many times the pay is better, the benefits better, the equipment better, and the runs better. The work may be a little harder but it usually is better due to the equipment. Don't get fooled into thinking you have it made until you have experienced a private carrier.

Working for that chemical company was exactly what I had been looking for up to that moment. We were paid well, were specialized in what we did, and were seen as the experts allowing us to prove ourselves and self-worth to the company. I enjoyed that type of operation because of the work ethic and I was brought up with a can do attitude. The good thing about working for a large company is that they see training as an important part of your development and as an investment for the company. Due to the nature of the products we were delivering there was training on an ongoing basis. I am always amazed when I hear that trucking companies have one or two safety meetings a year. Our safety meetings were eight hours per day or more and at least once a quarter. That was just on the basics of defensive driving and chemical delivery, however I found the training outside of those meetings to be what interested me the most. Now that I worked for an operation where I knew my schedule I started looking outside of the business for more training. I have always said you are dead in the water if you stop learning and many times high paying jobs with lucrative benefits can be the death of the employee. Although my goal was to move up in the company over time I like everyone else was enjoying that feeling of making it, I had a decent position with a good company and all the perks. I enjoyed being able to go home at five o'clock in the afternoons to see my family. The way our runs were set up I worked four to six weeks around town and switched with another driver to work out of town four to six weeks. Since we didn't work weekends it afforded me more time at home, which if you remember was my goal since the kids were born. I thought I had made it and was now looking at what else I can accomplish when one day the rug was pulled out from under me.

After three years with the company my wife and I decided to divorce. This time would be the lowest of my life and one that I would not wish on anyone, however sometimes bad times can be the jumping off points that you need to move forward. I won't go into the details but that period for me was a rough one that I didn't see coming. I view it now as a way of a higher power telling me it is time to rethink your life and boy did I ever.

Earlier I was just looking into some training for the future but going through some counseling I was urged to finish what I started. The first thing was to go back to school and get my diploma. I began taking some courses in the evenings and got my diploma also finding out how much I liked to learn.

I didn't know it but this would be the jumping off of my career. I took business and marketing courses, computers, anything I could that I thought would help me directly in my career. During my performance appraisals I would ask to take seminars outside the company on topics such as customer service and dealing with people. I took one seminar a year and with a good attitude started getting noticed by my peers. I have always told myself I never wanted to be driving a truck at the age of sixty-five. I don't know why, I know many drivers doing it, but I felt there had to be more to life than driving your whole life. If that is what you want to do then great, but for me I felt there was more, I just didn't know what it was. Now there are two ways to take a course, you can apply the knowledge gained during the course, or you can ignore the material and feel having the certificate in your file is enough justification. May I suggest you take the knowledge you have learned and apply it to your day to day activities? That is the true success of learning. I have seen employees use the tactic of gathering certificates just to bolster their file; it doesn't help them in the long run.

I have more rolls of certificates at home!

As I continued to take courses I started getting noticed by people in management and was offered more duties such as dispatching, dealing with vendors, and taking over different roles in the company within our team. The secret to getting things done is to being willing to work hard and to schedule yourself. For instance when I went back to school I was told I had to attend a certain number of hours per week in class. I knew I couldn't make all the hours required but knew I could have the work completed. I went and spoke to the instructor explaining that my job took me out of town most of the week and that my regular work week was 60 hours so attending class during the week wasn't going to happen. I did however promise that I would have the work completed on time the same as if I had attended the class. I was allowed as long as I didn't slip behind and continued to work my tail off to complete assignments. I would do my assignments at break times on the road, we used to stay in hotels overnight so while eating dinner and afterwards I would take my books and complete assignments. I even had waitresses and others commenting on my drive and how commendable it was at what I was doing. This was great for my ego and kept pushing me further into getting the work done well. That drive will attract people to you, employers and others that you deal with don't want to hear the problems, they want to know how you plan to fix them. That was a great time for me as I learned that I did enjoy learning and I have become a book worm ever since. Even this exciting time of my life began to cause major problems taking me into a tail spin again.

If you remember four of us started on the same day, we hired a couple more drivers afterward but the team was still relatively small. We all had the same amount of expertise, but one of the team members had done the same job with a prior carrier. We had always viewed him as the leader even informally. He knew the customers, most of the routes and was old enough to be seen as a mentor. There was one thing he didn't do however, he didn't upgrade himself. He didn't want to improve his computer skills; he had no interest in dispatching or making presentations for safety meetings, but enjoyed the background stuff. This was his downfall. It came to a point that a promotion was required within the team and one person would become the team leader. Viewing my friend as a leader already I gladly threw my cards behind him and said I would support him for the promotion.

In the end I received the promotion leaving a dark hole to be patched up that didn't go well. I was the youngest person on the team and was now in charge of ten people. As our team had grown all of our processes had become computerized and thankfully I had kept up with technology and embraced it. I turned out to be the only person qualified for the position out of the whole team. I tell everyone in my classes today that embracing technology and continuing to learn are your best assets in life. As mentioned before if you stop learning you die.

The next few years would give me growth like never before. As the years passed I became involved in more projects outside of the team and had a chance to travel more on business, like driving a truck is not traveling on business. I had the opportunity to help open new markets and delivery areas, create new teams and invest in new equipment. I had become the supervisor for the team and began to enjoy the corporate side of life. Many weeks I was in the office all week although my position required me to fill in when other drivers were on vacation or sick, it showed me another side of business. I was responsible for budgets, suppliers and making sure we were paid for the services we were providing. This intrigued me very much. I have always looked at myself as entrepreneurial and have tried everything from owning a truck to network marketing. The knowledge gained through being a supervisor was invaluable to me as far as learning more about business. I also continued taking courses from Health and Safety to Business and Customer Service. I still to this day try to take a course every year if possible. Corporate life went on like this for a few more years and although I was climbing the ladder I was starting to feel trapped. Our company was bought many times by other firms, reporting lines changed by the minute and as our team got larger things didn't seem to be getting any better. I found I needed a vacation all the time and myself and other supervisors were taking stress leaves like a domino board. The corporate culture was getting to me and things were not looking good. One day after a bad day at work I decided to take a bold move, a move I was hoping I would never regret.

Summary

Many people try too hard in the interview process or are ill prepared for what is required and blow their chance at a good impression. No matter what you think a truck driver should look like make sure you dress like the boss, a suit may be overkill, but a clean shirt and pants are important, cut your hair if required and look like a person that is a professional in the industry. There is a fine line between arrogant and knowing you have much to offer an employer so acting as if not needing the job sometimes is the best way to go. I didn't really want the job at the chemical company because I thought the spots had already been filled. This helped me not panic and remain calm through the interview process. Owning that professional attitude will attract companies to you instead of you hunting for them. Employers want leaders and professionals.

Once you get a good position in a company that may be a private carrier or a for-hire carrier that believes in the importance of training take advantage of it. I see employers that offer training to their staff and no one takes it on, thinking it is extra work. Think of it as an investment in yourself for the future. If you decide down the road to move into another position that training and information may be very valuable. Learn on your own, many folks when they land a good job feel they will be there forever and since they got the job on current credentials they don't need to learn anything more. Keep learning even if it is for your own development. Those who stop, die! The learning can be from books, courses, workshops, videos, audio tapes, and more.

The options are endless so there is no excuse for not learning even when driving down the road. As mentioned in my story of the promotion if you decide not to keep upgrading then people will pass you by for positions that should have been yours for the taking. Don't do that to your career, keep current and keep learning you will be glad you did in the end.

We all go through low periods and I am certainly no different from anyone else. I understand that they can feel life threatening but when you look back on them they may even be for the best. If I hadn't gone through a divorce I may not have gone back to school, I would not have met my current spouse that has supported me to no end and I may not be writing this book. If you are in a low period of your life get through it the best you can, seek help, find a friend, and do your best not to cause bigger problems than you have, but also look at what could be. I am not saying it is easy but you will get out of it and you can be successful at what you do. Work at it and you will get there.

I tell everyone in my classes today that embracing technology and continuing to learn are your best assets in life.

Chapter 6

Become an Ambassador for the Industry

It is important to remember where you came from and at the end of 2006 I made a bold move and left the company where I had been working as Supervisor of the fleet. Contemplating what I was going to do with my time and even more important, how I was going to get paid became the new focus of my days. The one danger that many drivers get into when working for long periods of time at good companies is that they forget where they came from. I found our team becoming like that, these were all experienced drivers and collectively we had much experience to share, but people were feeling entitled. For the last thirteen years our drivers had enjoyed expense accounts, hotels for sleeping in, freedom to do their runs how they saw fit, quality equipment, and good salary with great benefits. In a way it is almost like spoiling your child. I certainly won't disagree and say I didn't enjoy the perks but I remembered what I had done in the past and made sure not to abuse those lines in the corporate world. This is important because entitlement will cause you to stop working hard. This is because you have forgotten the past; you think the future is a piece of cake. Our team didn't even have to cross the border although we had all worked across North America, but I used to remember times sitting at the border waiting for customs many times for free. I remember some of the bad equipment I drove in the past and how I have worked hard over my career to always have each truck I drove looking its best.

Remembering your roots can humble you and make you even more important to the industry. More importantly, it can make you more tuned into your career. Remembering where you came from allows you to improve your own career, respect the perks that come with your position, and remember what it was like in the past so that you don't make mistakes that will take those items away. I see this in many owner operators that have decided that they only want to run in certain areas, yet they wonder why they are losing money. Once you become selective of what you want to do then you have lost the game, because you won't be willing to work hard for your career. If you need to be selective about your work at a company maybe you need to be more selective about the company you work for.

I got this scratch in Louisiana and this one.........

After a short break reviving myself and wondering what to do next I decided to ramp up my illustration business that I had started part time in 2003. I wanted control of myself and my future and did not want to hit my death bed wondering what if? Starting a business can be nerve racking and I had tried many before, but this would be different. With the support of my spouse we decided to go full bore. Six months later things started happening and to this day we are still operating the illustration business successfully. In 2009 I started the consulting side of our operation with the 30 plus years of experience I have in the industry.

When deciding what to consult on with people I sought out information from people I respected in the industry and many mentioned insurance or safety training and the like. I found however that wasn't me, when I looked back over my career what I did see was ambassadorship, leadership, and now business. You may be wondering what I mean by "Ambassadorship", but I've mentioned in past chapters how I used to keep my equipment, in the past I would pull into rest areas and park the truck and then have a bus load of visitors park next to the truck and want to take a picture. People from other countries don't see large equipment the way we have it here in North America and so they are often fascinated by the chrome, size, and amount of trucks on the road. So I would be happy to let them take a picture and even talk about where I go and so on. That happened to me many times and to colleagues I talk to as well. By letting them take a picture you have taken one step to becoming an ambassador for our industry. There is one secret to ambassadorship however, you have to have lived it. If you didn't keep your equipment in tip top shape, or you were always late at your customer delivery, or you couldn't hold a job it is very hard to become and ambassador to the industry. On the other hand don't go out of your way to become and ambassador, just do your best and the ambassadorship will follow. Ambassadors live their life, because at the end of your career or during it for that matter you must have a positive experience.

I was told early on not to get into the transportation industry by someone who had done it and quit. They didn't make any money, and here I have been in the industry for over 30 years and have always made money. Being a leader in this industry isn't hard, all you have to do is show up and be the best you can be, and even easier is the fact that there are so many people out there in the industry that don't care it makes you look good. You wouldn't believe the circumstances I have seen over the years of how people present themselves. Track pants and dirty shirts, profanity written everywhere and a total disregard for hygiene. I have seen drivers that go off the deep end with the customer if the load isn't ready, that won't make them welcome a second time. There are a host of other issues that are seen commonly across the industry that if drivers would just clean up their acts they would be so much better off. Every time I hear that drivers can't make money in this industry it is because they are doing something terribly wrong. The excuse you will hear is that, "Dispatch doesn't like me!" If you dig deeper in the situation the translation to that is," I have been late so many times that Dispatch doesn't trust me!" Very rarely have I sat in my career due to dispatch and if you ever sat in a dispatch environment you will understand they are not out to get the drivers, they need the drivers, they are making sure they have covered all the important loads and that is usually because some drivers are running behind. I understand the product may not be ready and other manufacturing or weather situations can create delays that are unexpected but very often delays are due to drivers with bad time management.

I decided that the leadership in the industry for some of the issues I just mentioned was the direction I wanted to go and there weren't many people talking about those issues. When I rolled out my consulting business I focused on business and leadership because I enjoy those things and working hard has got me to where I am in life. So what type of driver will you be? You may be starting out and not even know the answer to that question but it is important to think about. Are you the type to follow the crowd and have a mediocre career or be a leader and be willing to learn and do things the right way even if they cause you grief? I have talked about taking ownership of your position in the past; will you take ownership of your career?

The only one that can answer that is you. You can make money or lose money, you can be a successful driver, or an industry statistic, the choice is yours? I can't make that decision for you and no one can train you to be that person, it comes from inside. I can tell you this, if you're willing to learn, if you do your best to keep your image clean, you will succeed in the transportation industry no matter where your career goals take you. If you think this is a quick ride past steady work, or a quick way to get cash, then you have made a big mistake. This industry affects your whole life and how you wish to operate in it is your choice. You can sit on the edge of the water and read a book on how to swim, or jump into the pool and learn how to swim for survival.

I wish I could learn to swim!

Please don't come into this industry and be another piece of dead wood, we have many of those already. We need Ambassadors, we need people ready to stand up and make this industry work, we need people that will talk positively about the industry and give others a helping hand. If that sounds like something you will want to be part of then we welcome you aboard, if not, then there are plenty of other industries around that may be a better fit for you.

So how do you become an Ambassador to the industry? Don't worry there is no election, no board of approvals required. It starts with keeping your nose clean, keeping your record clean, both criminal and driving, and it means being a team player. Keep good time management skills, operate in a safe manner, help others when in trouble, keep your equipment in top shape, and be pleasant to be around. Once you have those basics you will find it very easy to be an Ambassador because people will look to you for leadership and responsibility. Once your company starts to depend on you, look at that as a good thing that means they trust you, that means your integrity factor is in sync.

I used to run New York and New Jersey on a regular basis and if you have ever been there it can be a hair rising experience. Add to the fact traffic and a dangerous environment and you will see why most drivers don't want to go there. The truth is there is nothing wrong with New York if you are careful, but most drivers don't even go that far. I was valuable to my company because I didn't give them a list of excuses and was willing to go they would give me my back haul ahead of time so I could plan my way out of the city. I got so good at New York I was able to go in one way and come out another end of the city saving myself toll charges, traffic congestion, and time. The company saw that I had the integrity to follow through and be on time.

When they tried that with other drivers, the drivers wouldn't call in to check in case a back haul had changed, some wouldn't call in at all. If you want to keep your career very short try that trick.

We had a driver that started with our company, brand new, he was on his first load and they sent him to New Jersey. This was a week when the weather was very bad, through the mountains of Pennsylvania the rain can get intense and weather can change on a dime. We had regular truck stops that we stopped at for fuel and as we all called in to dispatch for our daily checks they kept asking us if we had seen this driver. The reply kept coming back no. No one had seen his truck or driver all the way to New Jersey. After a few days of this things started to feel very wrong, had something happened, most of us had turned two trips by now and this driver hadn't even made it one way. Eventually this driver called in on the last day, his excuse was he didn't like to drive in the rain and it had rained all week. He had stopped at another truck stop that the rest of us didn't use very often and he didn't feel the need to call in until he delivered his load. His career ended very abruptly at our company. Even when things are going wrong have the decency to let people know what is going on and this is where many drivers fail. If you owned the trucking company and that was your customer you wouldn't be sitting in a truck stop all week waiting to deliver. Use your head in this industry and you will be miles away from everyone else. If you are serious about becoming an Ambassador, then start with a mission statement for yourself.

How many of the drivers on the road have a mission statement? How many know what a mission statement is? When I ask many of the students that are in my owner operator business class the answer often ranges from some sign they saw on the back of the wall in a warehouse to some company paragraph they were told to read when they started on with the carrier. Many of us don't take those statements to heart many times because they are written in a very corporate tone and many times don't include the very people that the mission statement affects. A business plan is a document that owner operators should be familiar with and the mission statement is the first item on a business plan.

So how can a mission statement apply to the owner operator or professional driver and why should we be concerned with it in the first place? As a driver the company you are hired on with is your customer, that is the most important customer in your business and how you treat them is a direct reflection on your business. Most owner operators or drivers do not realize the company is their customer. Most think that they are an employee of the company. They may be an employee but if you think of yourself as your own company you will be taking "Ownership of your position." Having a mission statement defines how you will operate your business and the type of operation you plan to operate. Your mission statement may include things like "I will provide on time delivery to our clients, be honest and true in the dealing with others, and offer the very best customer service available." Maybe your plan is to operate as a shoddy operator and your mission statement will include things like we will always look out for the work with the most dollar amount and are determined to win no matter what cost to humanity. A different type of company that may not be the kind of company I care to deal with but it is your company so it is your decision. The fact is that the mission statement is more for you than to paste on the wall of your garage. What type of driver do you want to be? Honest, operating with integrity is how I like to run my company and by having the mission statement helps keep those values top of mind. As I tell the students in my class the mission statement should be the first thing you think about as it defines the type of owner operator or driver you will be down the road.

Starting to think about professionalism directly out of the gate is a great way to start your career off in the right direction for a long successful future. If I can get one point through to you from this whole book, it will be become an Ambassador for this industry, not for us, but for you. A positive mind in this industry, coupled with a good work ethic will give you the basis for a great career in transportation. Transportation is a core industry and will always be around. It has never stopped and will never stop because it is the life blood of the economy. If you want a career get into transportation, but remember your name will stay with you for your entire career. We all make mistakes, we have all had things happen that we wish we could take back, but if you are honest, admit your mistakes, be willing to learn, and keep a good attitude, you will survive. That attitude will be the one thing that people remember throughout your career so make sure it's a good one.

If you need to be selective about your work at a company maybe you need to be more selective about the company you work for.

Summary

Millionaires often remember their days of poverty. Street kids often remember life before they hit it big with a musical record. You may not have hit success the way the stars have but if you have been growing in your career then you have been successful. The trick to remaining successful in the career that you chose is to remember the early days. Remember when you worked for companies that didn't treat you well and now you work for a company with many benefits and a kind soul? Remember when you would sit for hours at the border for free waiting for a clearance and your company has streamlined the process so you now roll through? Remember your early days and the price you paid and this will keep you humble. Being humble is the secret to making further gains in your career without taking people for granted.

At some point in every person's life they have to take hold of their career or business. Some decisions will be more drastic than others; it may be small decisions or a mountain of problems you have to weave through. It doesn't come easy. I am not suggesting that you take a drastic leap like I did and quit your job and start your own business, but you should always be looking to improve your career in some way. If you're happy where you are that's great, but if you settle into a safety net you will find that your career comes and slaps you from behind. It's kind of like when you were a child sitting in a big overstuffed chair that could lean back and forth and someone from behind comes and pulls the chair back making you almost fall out.

You didn't see them coming and many times when we get complacent in life we don't see problems coming and then the next thing we know we are handed a pink slip. Many people go through that in their careers. Take charge of your career even if it is going well and keep improving and learning allowing you to stay on the top of your game. Become an Ambassador for your industry. You don't have to become someone like Nelson Mandela but being proud of what you do and how you do it is the most important part. For instance you may be more comfortable in track pants and an old t-shirt but that doesn't look very professional. You may think that the appointment time dispatch gave you isn't important but you should still be there on time. You may feel that it is the company's responsibility to keep the trucks clean but you should wash it anyway. An Ambassador seeks initiative in their work; they have a sense of pride that makes them complete certain tasks because they care. An Ambassador has integrity and will be on time because that is what has been asked of them, not what they feel like doing. Ambassadorship is becoming the leader for your industry without being asked. Look for the Ambassadors that are already in the industry and see what they are doing. Who are they you ask? They are the Road Knights promoting safety, they are the top drivers at the company that don't squabble about loads, they are drivers that don't turn down work, they are the drivers that step up to the plate to get the company out of a tough spot, they are drivers that keep their equipment clean representing themselves and their company, they're on time, they're friendly, they're helpful, they're Ambassadors!

The real question is, will you be one?

Chapter 7
The Future of Trucking

I wasn't planning to write this chapter until a friend who took the time to review a chapter from the book suggested I include a chapter about the future of trucking. Do I know where trucking is going? Like any other industry professional I have mixed views as to where it should go, but I do know it has to go somewhere. As I write this book the industry is in the middle of a huge driver shortage that began in 2010 and has progressed to a point that may even put the economy in jeopardy down the road. I don't think there is a quick fix however, it's not like you can just shut down lanes, the wage environment won't change over night, and outside forces such as fuel prices, shipment charges, and insurance issues will always create complex issues for the industry. The industry has been around for so long and done things a certain way that changes will be met with much confrontation. As I was speaking with my friend about the book he began to mention that it is the driver that controls the state of the industry and the direction it goes.

To a point he is correct, we have let things happen to us such as running by the mile, and long work weeks because that is the way the industry was set up. The industry was set up to take the people that couldn't make it. You didn't need a university degree to get a job, it involved hard work the way our parents worked. Think about it, many of the drivers came from farms that had equipment such as trucks and tractors that they started driving at the ages of ten and eleven. Dad worked from 5:00am to 7:00pm at night tending the farm so working a twelve hour day holding a steering wheel was an natural step up in life. The other set of people other than the farm community was people like myself that didn't like school, and didn't know what we were going to do with ourselves. University wasn't looking like an option, unemployment certainly wasn't an option, so trucking looked fairly attractive. It had a low barrier of entry, it was performance based so the more you worked the more money you made, and the boss wasn't looking over your shoulder all day. Not a bad deal for people who didn't know what they wanted to do with themselves. Then there are the folks where our parents came to this country and didn't know anything about trucking. I fell into it by mistake out of just needing a job and managed to make it a great career. If you look at the people that came into the industry, the way the industry was set up, and the attractiveness of it at the time you will see why trucking worked for so many. It was the only way that we could make a career for ourselves out of nothing. I was pumping gas before falling into trucking. If I had taken a poll of my colleagues back in the day I am sure a good six out of ten drivers had a low education level, but hard work ethic. Many of my fellow drivers had never finished high school. That's why owner operators looked so good back then, it was the only way for someone to get into business for themselves with low capital and education. The industry has always been regarded as a dumping ground, the last resort for those that have failed at other careers or in education.

Things are changing however, although it is still regarded by many as the place of last resort, people are now realizing that the transportation industry touches everything in our daily life and without it the economy could shut down.

How do you go about changing an industry as old as the country is alive, operating the same way for as many years without grounding everything to a halt? Earlier my friend and I discussed it will come down to the drivers themselves and although I agree to a point I am not sure that is the whole story. It has been tried many times through strikes, petitions, and surveys and we hav-

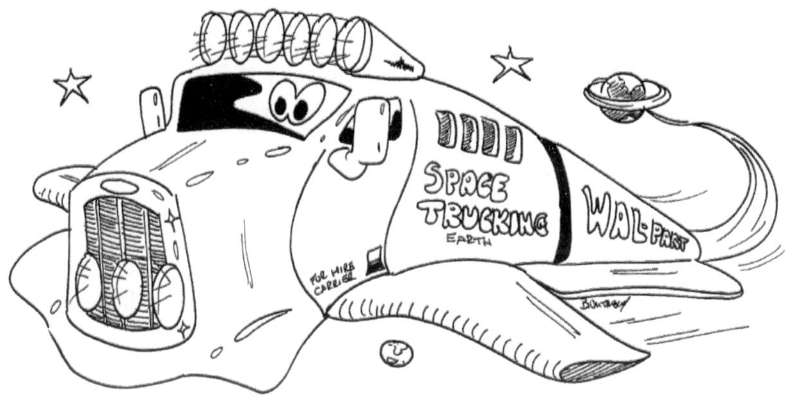

en't been able to change things to date. That's because people need to eat and support their families and though they agree with the idea getting the country together is another problem. I personally don't think that the drivers will be able to pull off the change required. They just don't have the authority in the right areas to make that change. In some industry seminars of late it has been mentioned that associations are the ones that should drive the change. I think they will be paramount for advocating for change, will be great for educating people on the changes, but at the end of the day they don't have the authority to make any changes either. Companies certainly won't be at the forefront to make the changes because it will hit them directly in their pocketbooks and some are just surviving as it is.

The change has to come from the top, it has to come from Government. Like the CEO of a corporation they are the only ones that have the authority to make those changes and mandate them down the line. The industry is talking about it right now, getting the professional truck driver designation as a skilled trade. This should have been done long ago and will be a huge step to getting us moving in the right direction. The rules and regulations that a professional driver has to know would floor the average person. Having a curriculum that shows a driver has achieved a certain level of achievement will give the driver a more educated forefront to make decisions on companies and will level the playing field for the good drivers. Paying drivers decently and getting away from the by the mile wage model will also go along way to setting up the industry to attract people to a driving career. The third piece is home or family time, there has to be a model where a driver can have a life off the road with family. I don't view the road time as bad myself and I don't think other drivers should either. I think that we need to look at a model much like some of the private carriers are doing. Working a set amount of days within a four day week, allowing a longer weekend, with family. Set work days and overtime after a certain point in line with other industries. I think the last part is to find a model where an owner operator can expand the potential of their earnings. Profit margins are low in transportation, there needs to be a way of increasing profits through a fuel management system through the country, higher freight rates, or some other incentive to attract business owners to the industry. We need to look at other industries and see what is attracting the young people and model some of our own processes after those programs. We want good safe drivers out there that are educated, we all want that. The question is how to do it without grounding the economy to a halt? That problem is yet to be worked out and we will see how it shapes itself for the future.

In the meantime we still need people in the industry and I myself still think it is a great industry to be in. Like any other industry it depends how you approach it, the type of person you want to be in the industry, and what you want to achieve. I think if people look at the industry positively, they may see what many of us see that have been in it for years. Take a look at the positive parts of the industry.

Many people think that the travel is a negative of the industry instead of a positive. Almost every industry from the finance industry, to marketing and sales, to material management, safety and transportation all travel heavily to achieve their goals. It may be for weeks at a time or systematically for conferences but every industry has travel associated with it. The CEO of a corporation travels for weeks on end, sales forces are on the road as much as truck drivers, material management positions may be required to travel between plants and or countries for extended periods of time. If you are trying to find a job that doesn't travel then I suggest looking at the fast food restaurant down the road for a position. Sales teams, CEO's, are in planes much of the time and see nothing from one stop to the next. They go to their hotel room, drink at the bar, and crash before their day of meetings. At least with transportation you see the country, you meet those folks in little pockets of the country that you can't even find on a road map. I have eaten some of the best food on the planet at some little food stops where you had to park the truck on the street. How many people that travel have gone canoeing in Florida, air boat sight seeing through the swamps of Louisiana, or seen the magnificent sunsets that happen on Interstate 10 in the South? How many positions allow you to talk to some of the nicest people I have ever met in small town Alabama, experienced the true beauty of the state of New York, or seen the magic of the ocean in Ft. Lauderdale Florida. You have to drive to see that stuff. My wife and I are still doing road trips to some of the cool places I have seen over the years and many wonderful memories come back on those trips. Don't hide from travel, embrace it, most people don't leave their hometown. There is nothing like the open road to help you appreciate the country we live in, see it for yourself.

The next issue that comes to mind from people investigating the industry are the long work hours. Transportation has a normal work week of 60-70 hours per week roughly six days a week. Those coming from a factory or manufacturing background may have a hard time adjusting to a long work week. The work week is set up like that in transportation for a reason. If we only drove eight hours per day you would never get anywhere and you certainly wouldn't make any money. The average driver should be able to achieve 500 miles per day if dedicated to their run.

Most destinations from Toronto Ontario to the high freight areas of the Untied States are within 500 miles. New York, New Jersey, Pennsylvania, Chicago, Indianapolis, West Virginia and more all are within range of driving in one day. Add in customs and other important stops along the way and it will require at least a ten hour day to reach those destinations. If you were unable to reach those destinations in one day and return the next there wouldn't be enough money in this industry to warrant drivers. The current set up allows for that 2000-3000 mile week that gives people the income required for success. If you look at people that work in manufacturing environments, landscaping, and other industries many times they are looking for overtime to supplement their wages. How many times have you had a friend say that a company cut their overtime and it will be a bad pay this month? How many people have you seen that have a full time job but also work a part time job on weekends. I know people that have been in the trades and either work the overtime and count it as their regular work week or are doing work on the side. I have family members that have been in the accounting field their whole lives and are always working extra hours to catch up on client work. I know trades that work 50-60 hours on a regular basis no matter how much money they are making. Those that have achieved a degree in the finance field or management may be working much harder than they thought to pay off the education they went through.

You'll need more than the money we pay you!

I know doctors that are working almost twenty hours per day. Most of us want to fill our time productively and while I do believe you need time off for recreation and family life I do think it is achievable in the transportation industry. It takes some planning and as I have said in other chapters making some personal guidelines will help you stay focused and on track. It won't matter what industry you are in there are long hours all over, but if you are doing something you enjoy, and have additional perks like seeing this great country we live in then it is all worth while.

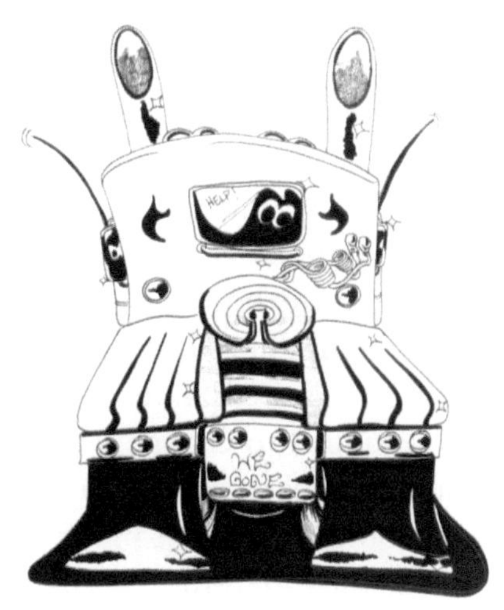

The issue of income is a big one for everyone, but really the industry doesn't pay that badly. What is hard for people to understand is the "by the mile" model that has been a long time staple of the industry, but is it really? The largest issue facing the industry as far as income is concerned is the wasted time. If a driver gets held up at a delivery dock they may be paid for the delivery at $25. That's okay if they are out within one hour which is a standard delivery time. What if they are held up for two or three hours, then that driver is earning a wage of $5 or $10 per hour. If dispatch has trouble getting loads organized then they are now impeding on your income. These are the areas of transportation that need addressing and will be addressed in the future. Finding a job that pays you $25 per hour is very hard to find, with the hours we work most drivers earn between $50-$70,000 per year depending on the operation they work for, and the best part is the work is always there. Transportation isn't seasonal, isn't affected by holidays, vacations, or business. It will dip with the economy and business to a point but for the most part it is a stable environment. The goal in the industry at this point in time is to make sure drivers are paid for their waiting time and right now that depends on the company you work for. The more you specialize in this industry the more you can earn so moving into specialized areas such as chemical delivery or flatbed can earn you even more money.

Summary

This is a time of change, I certainly don't have a crystal ball but the leaders of this industry are changing things in a big way. It began in the United States in 2010 and has continued to change across North America. The recruiting shortage has made some major flaws in the industry come to the forefront. As expenses like fuel, communications, and employees keep changing, ideas are coming forth to change the way business is currently done. The barrier for entry will rise as we change the way the game is played so a new driver may want to get in now while the barrier to entry is low. This industry will change for the better, it always does. What if it doesn't? I believe it will change but what if it stays the same? I believe it is still a great industry to be a part of, I have been in it since I was seventeen years old, have made great money, seen the country, and still continue to be part of the industry. The people I know in transportation have been there for a long time, that is because the industry is fun, filled with good people, and has a solid infrastructure. The industry has enough room for each person to be individual and not be stifled by company culture. If you ever wanted an office with a window, trucking is the perfect place for you, the windshields are getting bigger all the time. I would like to personally invite you into an industry that has great men and women involved, has been around since vehicles were made, and will be around for the future. I promise you, you won't regret it.

The barrier for entry will rise as we change the way the game is played so a new driver may want to get in now while the barrier to entry is low.

Acknowledgments

This book has taken 50 years to produce. No, I am not that slow of a writer, but I couldn't have written it 20 years ago, going through life creates character, it shapes a person, and it helps you grow. Without the experiences in my career good and bad, this book wouldn't have been possible. It is also without doubt that this book couldn't have been written without many of the people that I have met in my life. I make it a habit to try and learn from everyone that enters into my life whether it is a good or bad experience. It is like going to a seminar where you are told to take one thing home with you, or a movie where you remember one important scene, each person you deal with in life will offer you one aspect that only they can show you. Make sure you are learning from everyone you meet.

The first person that has to be acknowledged is my wife Carmen. She is my business partner, my wife, my friend, and probably most important of all my opposite. She has a way of supporting me while setting me straight and I value our time together like no one else, she offers great insight. My father introduced a great work ethic in my life as well as showing me the advantage of being friendly with other people. He never judged and I thank him for that. I have too many other people to thank so I will do that in one big swoop. There are many, because many of them may not even feel as though they did anything. Many have been former bosses such as my friend Gary who always instilled in me that, “knowledge is power”, my former partner Andre that gave me my first insight into the trucking business as a business owner, and the teachers that have inspired me to push further.

There are also those that inspired me in a negative way. The guy that told me don’t get into trucking, it would be a waste of time, that was 32 years ago. The driver from the moving company that kept pushing me to be better while making him more upset so much that he quit. There was my former boss that didn’t give us enough fuel money to make a simple trip to Windsor, Ontario allowing me the message of never running out of fuel again in my career. Also we need to recognize the teacher that gave me a poor mark in illustration allowing me to have a successful illustration business today. Also a giant thank you to those of you who said I couldn’t do it, “#$@&%* you!”

There is also a list of people who are mentors and may not even know it. My friend Yves who passed away too young and I greatly miss him and it taught me life is too short, my friend Kim whose advice I take to heart every day and envy his family life. Then there are the Dragon’s from Dragon’s Den who inspire my entrepreneurial spirit along with Richard Branson, Gene Simmons, Andrew Matthews, Alan Weiss, and many others that I follow. The list can go on from former colleagues to inspiring movies such as Pay It Forward.

I learn from everyone and if you plan on being around and being effective you need to learn from everyone as well. We are all shaped by the people we meet and learning from each of them is the best way to make the most of those relationships.

I hope you have enjoyed this book and will make the most of your career and your personal life. I wish you well and hope that you will use this book as a guide for inspiration to take a chance on fine tuning your career, improving yourself through education, and becoming the star of your industry. Life is too short, so make the most of it while you're here.

All the best,

Bruce

Profile

Bruce Outridge

Bruce's first look into the world of transportation began at the age of 17. He seemed to come into his own with the world of transportation. Starting in the moving industry anyone like Bruce was regarded as a prime candidate to carry furniture out of your house. He didn't come from a long line of truck drivers, in fact in his household nobody knew what a truck was. His Dad was a hard working accountant, his Mum worked for the airline. He just needed a job; there was no grand plan at that point. From day one in the industry he learned the importance of customer service; the public is good for that – training! His father brought him up with a great work ethic and that carried him through life to this day. He moved up the ranks and became a driver for the company eventually moving from Atlas Van Lines to North American Van Lines. As a driver he was paid a percentage for regional moves and learned the art of negotiating with helpers for pay, assessing costs for trips, and time management. He moved further into his career, got his "A" license and owned his own truck with a partner at the ripe young age of 20 years old. He decided to move to the freight side of the industry after a few years and started in the city. From there through a connection he started his highway career hauling magazines throughout the US for a private carrier.

He loved that job and finally felt his dream of working with the big trucks and all the chrome. After the company shrunk its fleet Bruce moved over to a smaller company where he learned the art of driver, dispatcher, and more. Unhappy there he began with a Burlington Ontario company and continued to run North America for the next six years. He enjoyed those years but kids came along and he found he wanted to be home more. An opportunity came up to run for a private carrier again and he joined the forces of a private chemical fleet. Having hauled chemicals for most of his career he was a good candidate for their fleet. Since they were regarded as sales his customer service skills moved him up the corporate ladder quickly finally arriving as Team Leader for the fleet. He flourished in that position but frustration with company policies caused him to leave after a 13 year employment with the company. He took the daring leap into entrepreneurship.

In 2003 he started an art business part time and after leaving his job in 2006 he decided to start Bruce Outridge Productions doing editorial illustration, cartoons, caricatures, and more. Realizing he enjoyed public speaking and having 25 years of knowledge that he could share with new drivers and owner operators he opened Outridge Consulting Services in 2009. Bruce spends time operating both divisions as needs arise. He absolutely loves being an entrepreneur, being creative, and helping people. After adding Outridge Translation Services with his wife Carmen's expertise they tied all the divisions' into their parent company Outridge Enterprises Inc. The businesses have since launched many products and services from cartoon strips for many of the industry magazines to on-line training for Owner Operators.

Today Bruce is a columnist and blogger for industry magazines and businesses on business and leadership. In 2011 he was honoured as a recipient of the "Trucking Ambassador of the Year Award" by the Road Today Media Group. Bruce has begun his career as an author with his three business books titled "How to Start an Artistic Business" for artists, Running By The Mile" for owner operators, and now "Driven to Drive" for professional drivers. In addition to writing Bruce is still taking commissions for his artwork and produces various cartoon books for the industry called "Hammer Down" with two issues available currently. Bruce always mentions when asked about slowing down what is scheduled for the future? His response is that he has too many ideas in his head and plans on being busy for a long time. People ask why he is still in the industry when he doesn't have to be. He says the answer is simple, "The people!" For more information on Bruce and his many endeavors visit his website www.outridge.ca or www.outridgeenterprises.ca.

Interview with the Author Bruce Outridge of Driven to Drive on next page

Interview with the Author Bruce Outridge of Driven to Drive

The Rear View Mirror interviewed author Bruce Outridge asking why he created his second book "Driven to Drive" for the transportation industry?

TRVM: Your book is for professional drivers in the transportation industry, but it also paints a picture of your career as a driver, why was it written this way?

Bruce: When I put together the book "Running by the Mile" it was focused on owner operators and based on many of my experiences talking with industry professionals and owner operators already in the business. I found there was a lack of the business sense for the industry, almost like it was this big black hole that no one was to talk about. With "Driven to Drive" I looked back at my career and thought why have I been so successful when others haven't? I found much of it is due to people not thinking about how what they do affects someone else. With the recruiting shortage in full swing the driver issue has come to the forefront and I feel we need to stop just filling seats, we need to make this industry a good place to go to work.

TRVM: You have been off the road for around seven years now and the industry has changed dramatically in that time, do you think your book is still relevant?

Bruce: Most certainly the book is still relevant. Some of the technology has changed and a few of the regulations have changed, but for the big picture the industry has not changed very much, especially in the areas that I discuss in the book. The book deals with issues like customer service, ambassadorship, how to deal with family life on the road, and also some of the mistakes I made early in my career that many new drivers will go through in their career. Those things don't change, they will always be required.

TRVM: You consider yourself an ambassador for the industry, why is that?

Bruce: I did win an award back in 2011 for ambassadorship, but that isn't why I feel I am an ambassador. I have just had a good positive experience in my career. I have made mistakes, I have had downfalls, but in the long run I have worked for good companies, made good money, and made many friends within the industry. I worked hard to keep equipment clean and give a positive outlook on the industry. I think any good driver is an ambassador, look at the Road Knights, award winning owner operators, or the Highway Angels, they are all ambassadors of our industry. That comes naturally from a good positive career.

TRVM: What message have you got for the future of trucking and the new people coming into the industry?

Bruce: David Bradley, and many other industry professionals have been talking about this through groups like the OTA and others, the fact that we need to make the industry inviting to new people and profitable for all. Reclassifying it as skilled labour will go a long way, but won't solve all the problems. People for years have been seeing the negative side of our industry and we need to show them the positive side. Show them the independence available, the potential of different fields in transportation, and why so many people are involved for a lifetime. We need to start screaming louder than the negative side, and that starts with each one of us.

TRVM: Bruce, thank you for your time and all the best on the new book. For more information visit www.outridge.ca

About the Author

The Rear View Mirror is an industry publication promoting recruitment, education, and advocacy for the industry. The publication is owned and operated by KRTS Inc. and is available on-line at www.therearviewmirror.ca

12 Points of a Professional Driver

If you want to have a great career as a professional driver work on these 12 points. Strengthen the ones that need improvement and you will have a great career.

◊ Patience (Have patience with others)
◊ Respect (Respect others positions)
◊ Ownership (Own your career)
◊ Friendly (Be friendly to people you meet)
◊ Equipment (Keep your equipment in top shape)
◊ Safety (Operate safely on the roadway)
◊ Strategic (Plan your trips for success)
◊ Integrity (Do what you say you're going to do)
◊ Orderly (Be neat and organized)
◊ Negotiable (Be a team player and work with others)
◊ Accountable (Operate drug and alcohol free)
◊ Licensed (Keep your license clean and up to date)

It's your career, create something great from it! No one else will!

www.ingramcontent.com/pod-product-compliance
Ingram Content Group UK Ltd.
Pitfield, Milton Keynes, MK11 3LW, UK
UKHW041934190726
13854UKWH00004B/1593